# Tom Wellner and *Leading with Humanity*

"The critical success factor in any business at any time has been and will continue to be talent. It's always been a constant that to win in business you need to win the war for talent. That's how truly great companies win—they attract, retain, and motivate great people. In this wonderfully expressive book Tom Wellner establishes just how you go about doing that. It's a practical guide to a great future. Read it, learn it, and employ its lessons."

**—Professor David R. Beatty**
*Director, The David and Sharon Johnston Centre for Corporate Governance Innovation, Rotman School of Management at the University of Toronto*

"Tom Wellner was a purpose-driven CEO long before it became trendy and mandatory for companies to have a purpose greater than making money. He was there not just at the creation of the biggest revolution in business in many generations; he was there before the creation. *Leading with Humanity* shows how being human and making profits aren't mutually exclusive. If anything, they rely on each other."

**—Bob Ramsay**
*President, Ramsay Inc.*

"In *Leading with Humanity*, Tom Wellner describes why authentic, humanistic leadership is essential in crisis management. Genuine concern for clients, families, and team members is foundational to developing the best response to unexpected challenges. Wellner learned and exemplified this principle during the toughest times of the pandemic. Readers will benefit from his well-told stories and insights."

**—Dr. Bob Bell**
*Professor Emeritus, University of Toronto; Former Deputy Minister, Ontario Ministry of Health*

"As the economy of North America has been transformed from a goods-based one to a service-oriented economy, the management books that sit on our shelves touting 'more widgets for less' through autocratic management have become irrelevant. This fascinating book by one of Canada's great business personalities tells how to apply humility, kindness, and creative adaptiveness to achieve greatness. It shows that even in a once in a century crisis, those principles work to bring success. I'm sure this will become required reading at business schools, but it should be a must-read for all young people facing a changing and challenging world."

**—Dr. Calvin R. Stiller**

*Corporate Director; Professor Emeritus,
University of Western Ontario; Member of the Order
of Ontario, Officer of the Order of Canada*


"I found Wellner's writing to be superb and the stories enlightening and valuable for anyone contributing to today's workplace."

**—William J. Ringo, Jr.**

*Mentor and Chair, numerous Biotech Boards*

"Wellner is the type of leader who stops at nothing to protect and care for his people, his customers, and his community. Yet, he is humble enough to share some of the great life lessons he has learned during his successful career. *Leading with Humanity* is a must-read textbook for the modern leader and a reminder of the timeless importance of servant-based leadership."

**—Ali Shivji**
*Principal, Optima Living*

"Tom's concept of achieving the balance between human dividends and financial dividends for an organization is one that our new COVID-19 world could hugely benefit from. This is a perfect read for students in our global business schools. Tom's approach is refreshing and energizing."

**—Beth Oakes**
*Managing Partner and Executive Coach, The Oakes Group*

"As CEO of Revera, Tom Wellner was in the eye of the COVID-19 storm. In the face of severe adversity, he managed Revera with great compassion. In *Leading with Humanity*, Tom provides the lessons he learned: how to skillfully manage a business while acting in a manner that is consistent with the core values of inclusivity, teamwork, care, grace, and sensitivity. Tom has a compelling perspective on balancing these potentially conflicting objectives. It should be required reading for entrepreneurs, business professionals, and business students."

**—Steve Mayer**
*President, Greenhill Canada*

"Today's business leaders are faced with the challenge of leadership in a post-pandemic world. Tom Wellner's book is arriving at the perfect time. His years of experience at Revera will greatly benefit those in need of up-to-date advice."

**—Hazel McCallion**
*Former Mayor, Mississauga*

"What's the secret to leading through turbulent times? Tom Wellner's *Leading with Humanity* serves as a blueprint for leaders looking to create high performance standards while engaging and inspiring their teams during periods of tremendous change."

**—Janet Ko**
*Communications Executive*

Tom Wellner's book describes and exemplifies the entrepreneurial spirit I was privileged to know at Eli Lilly. Well into his career, Tom still listened, learned, and led to the benefit of the residents, clients, partners, and investors.

**—Richard Pilnik**
*Eli Lilly Executive (retired)*

# LEADING

# WITH

# HUMANITY

*How Purpose Creates Value*

# LEADING

# WITH

# HUMANITY

TOM WELLNER

**Forbes** | Books

Published by Forbes Books, Charleston, South Carolina.
Member of Advantage Media.

Forbes Books is a registered trademark, and the Forbes Books colophon is a trademark of Forbes Media, LLC.

Printed in the United States of America.

10 9 8 7 6 5 4 3 2 1

ISBN: 9781950863310 (Hardcover)
ISBN: 9781955884587 (eBook)

LCCN: 2022919641

Cover design by Megan Elger.
Layout design by David Taylor.

This custom publication is intended to provide accurate information and the opinions of the author in regard to the subject matter covered. It is sold with the understanding that the publisher, Forbes Books, is not engaged in rendering legal, financial, or professional services of any kind. If legal advice or other expert assistance is required, the reader is advised to seek the services of a competent professional.

Since 1917, Forbes has remained steadfast in its mission to serve as the defining voice of entrepreneurial capitalism. Forbes Books, launched in 2016 through a partnership with Advantage Media, furthers that aim by helping business and thought leaders bring their stories, passion, and knowledge to the forefront in custom books. Opinions expressed by Forbes Books authors are their own. To be considered for publication, please visit **books.Forbes.com**.

*I would like to dedicate this humble effort to each of my teachers, coaches, supervisors, and bosses over the years. Each of you has been instrumental in providing me with exemplary leadership roles to model.*

*I would like to thank my wife, Mary, whose bravery and unwavering support has enabled our family to experience more of the world.*

# CONTENTS

# Be Good and Do Right

As the Irish organizational and leadership coach Orla Scott has said, "Purpose, people, and profit are not mutually exclusive." That's a belief I share, one that has guided my career choices and is reflected in my approach to leadership. It is a belief that I am mindful of as I start each workday, for I want to lead businesses that treat people—customers, team members, and other stakeholders—as humans, recognizing their dignity, treating them with respect, and demonstrating that I value them. I also want to lead businesses that try steadfastly to contribute to the greater good even as they achieve business sustainability. I'd go a step further. I don't think you can run a business that loses sight of its people or its purpose without having it become soulless, and I'd question if a soulless business can retain customers or talent. Losing either is a death knell for profitability and longevity. I think it is human nature to want to find gratification at work and to invest in enterprises that are intent on accomplishing a meaningful purpose while providing quality financial returns. Certainly, the board members I've been privileged to work with at several companies have proven that to be true, as have countless team members who regularly demonstrate that meaningful service fuels them with energy and a sense of value beyond the basic necessity of a pay cheque.

The reality of running a complex organization is that we have to balance profit and purpose. Leaders' decisions always have human consequences. If we are to lead with humanity, we have to take pains to consider the human impacts of the difficult business decisions we make. We also must make certain that the actions resulting from such decisions are implemented in a respectful manner aligned with the purpose, values, and culture of the organizations we lead.

Currently, I am the CEO of Revera Inc. Today, our company provides care and accommodation to twenty thousand seniors in long-term care homes and retirement residences in Canada and to forty-six thousand seniors in congregate settings across the United States and the United Kingdom. At Revera, our purpose is to make sure that the highest quality of life is considered paramount at any age and under every circumstance. Given the diversity of the residents we serve and the breadth of services with which we assist them, the work we do can be challenging.

The senior sector is no different from any other in that it requires leaders to make highly consequential decisions in quickly changing market conditions. Often decisions are forced upon us because of externalities beyond organizational control, and the impacts of our decisions can have harsh consequences on our people and profits, sometimes simultaneously. Finding equilibrium between the needs of the business and the impacts on people's lives is never easy, and there is no magic formula for such decision-making. Yet if we tip the balance scale too far in either direction, the consequences can topple the entire organization.

You may already have noticed I have referred to those Revera serves as residents. That in itself is a purposeful aspect of human-minded leadership. While you likely refer to those you serve in your own industries as clients or customers, throughout this book I will consistently refer to the people Revera or any of our operating brands serve as residents, for the retirement and long-term care residences we manage are their homes, and our frontline team members become part of their extended family. Because my industry is one where we share intimate relationships with our residents, it is easier than most, I presume, to focus on alignment with our purpose and to keep the impact of business decisions on people close at hand. Of course, our business is still a business, and the day-to-day organizational, financial, and logistical demands are as challenging as any corporation of similar scale. At Revera, considering all stakeholders goes far beyond shareholders and residents. In our case that includes numerous operational and capital partners and companies in which we have invested. We have developed a large number of joint ventures that are a central dynamic to our business strategy and that necessarily guide both human and financial obligations. Recognizing their needs and interests is vital to decision-making at Revera, just as is doing so for our team members, for decisions create chain reactions that percolate throughout an organization. Demanding? Of course. Yet it is in the marriage between business demands and people's needs—those of all our stakeholders—where I find guidance for the decisions I must make as a leader and where I turn in order to connect what can seem abstract strategies to concrete outcomes.

The reality is that even the most complicated parts of leading a business would be manageable if there were no humans involved. We can streamline processes. We can program machines and develop terrific software. We can employ data to analyze profitability and identify market opportunities. But whether "managing" our team or supporting our residents in their pursuit of joyful, fulfilling postretirement lives, the human factor of our business offers the strongest challenges, the greatest surprises, and ultimately the most satisfaction.

Because people are diverse and because their lives are dynamic, we must become leaders who adapt efficiently to changing circumstances and who innovate when problem-solving. Smart leaders know they always must have a plan B in their back pocket for when circumstances change, deals fall through, stakeholders change their minds, or a crisis suddenly looms. The smarter leaders are ready to pivot as unpredicted events warrant and turn rapidly to plan C or plan D when necessary. Tough problems are going to arise. They are part of the landscape. Difficult problems and unforeseen circumstances require creativity and agility in our thinking and will make us imagine innovative solutions. This ability to manage the unknown also requires resilience. Because it's human nature to change, there will always be pressures for businesses to adapt. The ability to adapt and to do so quickly when changing economic conditions or other forces require it is a hallmark of modern business.

Sometimes those changes are as sweeping as they are unexpected. The unforeseen really can bloom into a full-scale crisis at what seems a moment's notice. As chance would have it, I started writing this book just before the global coronavirus pandemic began spreading around the world. We all had our lives and our businesses rocked by COVID-19, but as a leader in the senior services industry, at Revera, we were quite literally placed on the front lines of the pandemic, faced with decisions that had life-and-death consequences. COVID-19 wasn't only *the* crisis of my professional life span; it was the greatest healthcare crisis any of us have faced in a century, and it brought the interconnection of business, purpose, and people into stark relief. The human-minded approach to leadership that we have developed at Revera was key to our ability to make decisions that reflect our purpose and meet the needs of our people while sustaining our business. We have been intentional at Revera in developing transparent, deep, and trusting relationships with our board, shareholders, and capital partners. That intentionality produced a larger culture that was quick and earnest in supporting the decisions we needed to make to do the right thing for our residents.

This is not a book about the pandemic nor is it about leading in times of crisis; it is about human leadership that balances purpose with humanity. But it does occasionally draw on the pandemic and Revera's response for examples and illustrations, and it does advance my beliefs about the qualities that are essential to creating workplace cultures that are resilient, agile, and innovative. These are the corporate attributes that serve companies well in good times and in bad. Yet I cannot ignore that this pandemic has tested my beliefs about leadership and corporate culture and reminded me why my career has taken the path that it has. You likely experienced something similar, for the pandemic caused us all to re-examine what we value and prioritize in our lives. I lost a grandmother in the COVID-19 year I spent writing this book, and more recently, my mother. The emotional void of being unable to comfort my grandmother in person as she passed, or to celebrate her life together with others, has been painful. My experience of this personal loss added to the empathy and huge respect I have always had for our residents, for their families, and for the frontline staff who support the seniors who call Revera home. I'm extraordinarily proud of those in leadership roles throughout Revera, at the support office, in our international platforms, and in all of our residences. Seeing their dedication to our residents and our team members was inspiring. They filled me with confidence that the belief systems we use to guide decision-making and the corporate culture we have tried to instill throughout the organization have paid tremendous dividends.

Not to be overlooked, those dividends have extended to our larger corporate culture belief in treating all people with respect and dignity. The importance we place on human value makes Revera a place where we are proud to work and where we are regularly rewarded by the wonderful intangibles of working with and alongside inspiring people. We benefit, as do our residents, by seeing one another as unique individuals with widely diverse experiences and interests who live engaged, dynamic lives.

The chapter divisions I have created not only convey the core structure of this book but also reflect the interconnected values I've spent my professional career developing as a leader. They are a true intersection of human-minded principles that can guide leaders about what is required to create efficient, effective, forward-thinking enterprises. By sharing examples from my experiences running several companies and working with excellent teammates and board members, I hope to inspire ideas for how you can shape your own company into one that is capable of resilient agility and equilibrium between balance sheet returns, team happiness, and customer satisfaction, all while achieving your guiding purpose.

One of those core principles I've already introduced is organizational agility. The ability to adapt as needs require starts with creativity. Creativity, which stems from leveraging inquisitiveness and fostering ingenuity, in turn gives rise to innovation. We're never going to be competitive if we can't work with our teams to find innovative solutions to problems. It takes effective problem-solving to grow a company, and in order to scale a business, we need to create workplaces that are intentional in balancing the strength of institutional resiliency with the agility to move fast. This in turn requires that we become outstanding at communicating, internally and externally, about the state of our organizations and our decisions. Central to clear communication is an ability to listen to our team members at every level, to value their input and ideas, and to credit their contributions and to extend our ability to hear and respond to similar contributions from other stakeholders.

Building a resilient, agile, purpose-driven culture where people want to accomplish good things for others, even when no one is looking, starts with us, at whatever level we provide leadership. Accomplishing these demands doesn't mean changing our nature; it means never forgetting our roots, our core values, and our natural curiosity. It means making sure that the culture we develop at work reflects the best parts of who we are and where we come from. When the companies we lead need to change to remain competitive, it doesn't have to come at the expense of our humanity. My own approach is to focus on taking the actions that will make the people who mean the most to me proud—people like my wife and children, my parents, my grandparents, and the teachers and mentors and coaches who helped shape me. Recalling how much I owe others keeps me humble. Trying to see the world through the experiences of others allows me empathy. Those are two traits I have found central to my roles as a leader. Empathy for others has helped me develop the tools to be more honest with myself. In my experience, good leaders tend to be humble. They are grateful for what their careers have allowed them to experience and appreciative to work among others who demonstrate passion and commitment. Humility fuels a desire to never stop learning and supports me when I make mistakes, acknowledge those mistakes, and then find the means to remedy them. I've made my share of mistakes. You will too. If you are committed to learning from them, they'll provide some of the most important lessons you'll ever learn.

Learning happens everywhere if we embrace it. The various leadership roles I've held over the past decades have challenged me

**Learning happens everywhere if we embrace it.**

to learn new lessons and take on new challenges. Throughout my career I have applied and adapted what I've taken away from my diverse experiences and the leaders I have had the pleasure of working with on management teams, the front lines, or with board members and shareholders. I credit my hunger for learning as the quality that has allowed me to see the importance of these other principles like resiliency, agility, balance, humility, and honest, transparent communication.

This book isn't about imposing any set of values on you. When it comes down to it, what I'm suggesting is that we are wise to remember the basic rules we learned as children—respect each other, listen, and be kind. In the way that as kids we were taught to play nice, share, and include one another, we need to apply adult versions of these rules and make sure we show respect for views that are different from our own, whether interacting with our colleagues or our customers, and make certain that everyone's voice is heard. We need to create cultures where people feel safe challenging the status quo, businesses where people ask questions and share ideas. When we create climates where we look after the people we serve, they also look after us and the interests of the business, and it is only in such climates that new ideas can produce new solutions and new opportunities. If we don't, our ideas become stale, infighting ensues, teams fall apart, and people begin only showing up for the pay cheque—such environments are debilitating and inevitably change the experiences of customers and clients as well.

This book is my humble attempt to share my thoughts and experiences. It's about never being satisfied with how things are and always looking for ways to improve. The way to evolve—and in business, if we don't grow and transform, we become irrelevant—is to search continuously for new tools and new ways to do things. If we don't, we are pushed aside by competitors and passed over by shifting markets. It is a book about leadership and life, and it tries to offer ways to balance what can seem to be competing demands:

**The way to evolve—and in business, if we don't grow and transform, we become irrelevant—is to search continuously for new tools and new ways to do things.**

- We can foster individual, inquisitive minds and still interact with and learn from others.

- We can learn to retain the best from the past and still remain relevant for the future.

- We can apply inquisitive thinking and original problem-solving in order to meet a crisis when it arrives *and* avoid the next crisis by planning for a future we can't yet see.

I hope that by the time you reach the end of this book, you will agree that we can create work cultures where we respect the people we serve and still attain sustainable economic results.

I hope that by hearing some of the stories from my varied career and about the passion I have for people-centred, innovative solutions, you can discover your own opportunities to transform the organizations you lead. And I hope that you will see that you can have a lot of fun along the way.

CHAPTER 1

# Stay Strong, Stay Focused: Leading through Adversity

Clare Hildebrandt, a former executive director of one of Revera's long-term care homes in Alberta, created a series of paintings titled *The COVID-19 Series* at the height of the pandemic. This series of images and accompanying text emerged from an abstract art class she took over Zoom in September 2020 and was inspired by the experience of working daily with residents during an early COVID-19 outbreak. Clare would be quick to say that she is not classically trained as an artist, having worked across the health system from pediatrics to geriatrics, and holding a master's degree in epidemiology, yet her art and accompanying descriptions convey so many of the complexities of COVID-19 in the unique environment of senior congregate living. Facing the crisis through endless days of uncertainty, challenge, and loss, Clare used art as a means to reflect on the pandemic and the intimate nature of working with our residents. Here is part of the text Clare wrote to accompany one image:

> **Dig Deep.** You never know how strong you are until you are in a situation where you have to dig deep. Resiliency is practiced in times of adversity. When feeling over-whelmed by a mountain of COVID, we figured out what one thing we could do next and did that, and then the many things that followed day after day after day.[1]

In this passage, Clare not only describes the tools needed to survive the overwhelming pressure to keep residents safe in the presence of a deadly disease but also captures the spirit any leader must embody in a time of adversity. No leader, and no organization, will emerge from crisis stronger unless they consistently demonstrate resiliency.

While it is true that we often marvel at the fortitude shown by those we come to regard as heroes, like Clare and all of Revera's frontline team members, it is a trait that can be learned and that can be cultivated within an organization. To some degree, resiliency can even be built into strategic plans. Acting with resilience when adversity arises will require individuals to dig deep within themselves, but they have a better opportunity to overcome difficult circumstances

---

1    Visit TomWellner.com to view the images by Clare Hildebrandt described in this chapter.

when the larger organization of which they are a part has intentionally built into the culture the traits that service resiliency—agility, innovation, transparent communication, team member empowerment, and focus on mission—and consistently reinforces them. Smart companies invest in good risk management strategies, and such traits can become focal points of that development. As leaders we hope we will never have to put these strategies to use, but as we all know a black swan event like a global pandemic can very quickly kick these strategies into gear and focus the organization's energy. It is an examination of these traits that makes up the focus of this book. I open here with a central theme on leading through adversity because events like we all faced with COVID-19 cement why these traits matter the most. Development of such qualities within your organization is what will carry you through the next crisis. That development can start by learning lessons from this once-in-a-lifetime event.

## Learning Lessons from Adversity

Early in January 2020, I met with our senior leadership team in the boardroom of Revera's Mississauga, Ontario, head office to prepare for our annual risk management review exercise. Like a corporate fire drill, the review involves an assessment of our readiness in the face of hypothetical events or situations that might impact our business operations—including a pandemic. Little did I realize at the time that just a few weeks later we would kick off our live pandemic preparedness plan in real time. Based on the COVID-19 experience in Asia and Europe, as well as what we'd learned from SARS nearly two decades ago, we focused our efforts on doing our part to protect Canada's hospitals, given the understandable concerns that they might run out of beds, ventilators, and overall surge capacity.

As a result, during the initial phase of the pandemic's first wave, we relied on public health directives and our normal influenza outbreak protocols to screen and restrict entry into our communities. At that time, we believed these measures could block the introduction of this new pathogen and control its spread. We now know that community spread and asymptomatic transmission had devastating effects. In the trying months that followed, we—alongside the rest of the world—learned a great deal about the challenges of containing this highly infectious virus, lessons that have come by way of so much mental and economic hardship and a tragic loss of life around the globe. In Canada, we now know that most of the country's initial COVID-19 deaths occurred among seniors living in congregate centres. It is a painful reality that has pushed many urgent questions to the forefront.

At Revera, we felt compelled to review why the pandemic had such a lamentable impact on the lives of our residents and staff in its first wave. Its toll on our frontline care teams and the grief we shared with residents and their families drove us to take extraordinary steps of self-reflection. Among these was the decision we made in early June 2020 to engage a diverse panel of independent experts to explore what happened in our homes during the first wave and how we could prevent the pandemic from causing further suffering in the next waves. As the second wave loomed, we chose to open our internal files and data to outsiders—almost in real time—so that the solutions they prescribed could be applied immediately to counter the ongoing threat.

The kind of purposeful reflection embodied by Revera's Expert Advisory Panel (EAP) and the Revera pandemic report that emerged from its diligent work reveals central corporate traits required for successful, purpose-driven organizations. We believe its findings were so important that we didn't just share them with colleagues in our industry, but we also made the final report public; indeed, you can access it on our corporate website. Not every situation warrants it, but I believe such transparency is an important part of doing good, and sharing our findings reflects our larger purpose of standing by our residents and improving the lives of seniors generally. There are some lessons worth sharing even in a competitive environment. In this case, the analysis and reflection can potentially save lives, not just from further waves of COVID-19, but it can potentially stave off the worst impacts of future viruses and better protect our residents from seasonal infection transmission. Turning intentional reflection into near- and long-term future action is the core philosophy of a successful corporate culture.

For the interests of this book, there are an abundance of lessons in our response to assessing how we managed COVID's first wave. You have already encountered two key traits: a dedication to strategic risk management planning that imagines potential future challenges and mechanisms for deliberate reflection that create lessons for the formation of evolving best practices. No doubt you experienced these needs in 2020 as well, for one thing about a global pandemic is that it's the great unifier—every business and every person had major parts of their lives upended. The specific examples I draw from Revera's COVID-19 experiences may not directly parallel your business, yet certainly the leadership approaches impacting actions behind those experiences can apply in any business environment. We'll never learn to predict the future perfectly. But we can learn from the past and we can get better. We'll never fix everything. If there is anything to be gained from this tragedy, it is the opportunity to learn from the forces that shaped it.

Your experience leading a business or a team during the pandemic probably shared many similarities to ours, including staff shortages, product procurement difficulties, and infrastructure and process challenges to meet safety protocols, among others. As a business on the front lines where the greatest suffering occurred, the pandemic placed other past experiences we once believed to be "crisis events" in a new perspective. We discovered one of the frustrating realities of the COVID-19 pandemic is that no management team, no matter its commitment or its quality, could prevent this virus from getting into a seniors' home if the disease was already highly prevalent in the communities where staff live. That reality was an important contributing factor for why the EAP titled their final report *A Perfect Storm*. We were at the storm's eye. According to the National Institute on Aging, between March and September, COVID-19 killed more than seven thousand Canadian seniors living in long-term care homes, accounting for nearly 80 percent of the country's deaths—a proportion far higher than other wealthy nations in the Organisation for Economic Co-operation and Development. Well before the pandemic struck, families of long-term care residents, unions, and industry associations across the country had been advocating for more funding to address staffing and infrastructure challenges in long-term care, including a shortage of physicians. But long-term care in Canada is not a sector that can operate in a silo. Private, not-for-profit, and municipal operators must rely on critical investment, input, and cooperation from across the health system to function well. COVID-19 exposed not only the cracks within the sector but also the broken links between it and the system as a whole. This translated into a series of systemic breakdowns that allowed the virus to flourish in long-term care. Among these breakdowns was a sector-wide shortage of personal protective equipment (PPE) to shield staff and residents from contracting and transmitting infection, along with a woeful lack of laboratory testing throughout the pandemic's first wave to identify those who were infected.

At the outset, it was not understood that asymptomatic individuals could spread the disease, nor that symptoms could vary so dramatically. Managing outbreaks within residences was further complicated by inconsistent and sometimes conflicting instructions from public health authorities. The pandemic exacerbated the sector's preexisting problems and historic challenges, including outdated long-term care facilities with multi-bed shared rooms and communal bathrooms that fueled the spread of COVID-19. As the pandemic stretched on, the sector's shortages of personal support workers and nurses intensified and challenged the industry's efforts to contain the spread of the virus. Health authorities in various regions discouraged the transfer of infected residents to emergency departments so that local hospitals could maintain their capacity to admit COVID-19 patients from the community. Simultaneously, the majority of necessary assets were directed to hospitals. There was also load shifting done to enable our hospitals to operate at lesser capacity to prepare for the potential surge of patients who did not arrive in Wave 1. Yet it was well known from the outset that seniors, with their advanced age and proclivity to have existing health concerns, were at high risk of the worst outcomes.

These were among the problems unearthed by the EAP's analysis. But, importantly, *A Perfect Storm* didn't stop at identifying the factors that made conditions inside many long-term care residences so dire; it offered specific, actionable recommendations. Creating mechanisms that provide intentional learning opportunities is critical to any business, but doing so is only a first step.

# Strategic Crisis Management

How do we go about applying our learnings in times of crisis?

*Insatiable knowledge appetites and open minds*: First, as leaders we must create cultures where the desire to apply learnings becomes locked into the cultural DNA. That starts by looking for a number of traits within the people we bring onto our teams and that we cultivate within ourselves. This ability to discover lessons from our experiences and from discoveries made by other thinkers starts with an insatiable hunger to learn. The EAP makes an excellent model for such behaviour. Virtually all of the participants on the EAP not only were experts in fields that offered a specific, informed perspective on infectious disease, design, and emergency response but also were individuals capable of thinking beyond their niche expertise and synthesizing the interconnections across disciplines. Leading an organization through the unknown requires depending on people who possess open minds and who become excited by new and challenging ideas. You need those who can see their way through big problems and discover innovative solutions to inform their analysis. The members of the EAP represented such traits, for they are the sort of leaders and experts who are receptive to compelling data and are skilled critical thinkers. Collectively, the group valued science and sought hard data before making their independent recommendations.

Here is a compelling example of the kind of thinking the EAP employed in their analysis. Because they are accustomed to applying a breadth of knowledge and pursuing the facts that emerged from multiple sources and differing angles of vision, they were quick to understand that the data available even quite early in the pandemic indicated specific causal patterns. Their applied critical thinking revealed gaps in decision-making and communication between the officials responsible for pandemic management and the various sectors best positioned to take actions that would protect a vulnerable industry. Their investigation understood the implications of the following timeline. Echoing the stance of the World Health Organization, Canada's chief medical officer of health recommended on March 30 that masks be worn only by the sick or those caring for them. However, reflecting the ever-evolving nature of scientific discovery, just one week later, the federal government reversed its guidelines on masks. Enough research had accumulated to prove that asymptomatic and presymptomatic people could transmit COVID-19 and that masks could be an effective aid in helping reduce transmission. Universal masking became mandatory in Ontario long-term care homes on April 8, yet same-day delivery of PPE to long-term care homes did not take effect until April 13. By then, COVID-19 had gained a strong and stubborn foothold in long-term care homes across the country. Revera's data shows that 97 percent of its residents' infections in long-term care in Wave 1 could be traced back to outbreaks that occurred during the week of April 13 or earlier. The same timeline applies to 90 percent of infections among its staff. Since only essential caregivers were permitted at long-term residences after March 9, the EAP found that the virus was most likely introduced into homes by staff members and essential caregivers who had contracted the infection in their communities. But in March, infected staff members without symptoms, or those who were presymptomatic, had little reason to suspect they were carriers and appropriately went to work, often unprotected. Meanwhile, public health officials did not prioritize long-term caregivers or residents for COVID-19 testing in March and April.

This is, on its surface, an example for how policy announcements and priority placement significantly worsened the sickness and mortality rates among seniors, yet it also offers a primer on how the power of factual findings, critical thinking, and purposeful synthesis create a path to understanding that has enormous implications for learning and future planning. While we might well expect this style and level of thinking from a panel of this nature, we've got to build these same thinking qualities into our teams, something the early chapters of this book will address directly.

Sharing some of the recommendations reached by the EAP is also instructive about the nature of applied learning that can guide a business forward. Here's one very straightforward recommendation from the EAP report: "A several-day supply of PPE must be maintained at every long-term care home. Central regional inventories should be established to provide supplementary supplies for homes that require extra supplies during an outbreak." More revealing is the Revera response, which implemented the specifics of the recommendation and now warehouses a six-month supply. We were also a founding member of the Canadian Alliance to Protect and Equip Seniors Living (CAPES), a volunteer-based initiative created by larger operators early in Wave 1 of the pandemic that sourced, supplied, and shared PPE across the seniors' living sector. CAPES was pulled together quickly by private sector organizations when we recognized the government had dropped the ball on PPE. The Canadian government had shipped PPE to China in January 2020 to help them manage their COVID-19 outbreak, and at a provincial level, all governments hoarded PPE for hospitals. The private sector stepped in to solve the problem for small operators that did not have the financial means to meet inflated PPE costs or the in-house skill set to locate needed supplies. Revera was shopping for PPE around the globe, leveraging the experience of our supply chain director, who had a lot of connections in Asia and Europe. By buying millions of dollars of PPE through this consortium, we drove down the cost of PPE and made it affordable for small operators. CAPES is an example of how, in crisis, you do the right thing.

Many of the EAP recommendations focused on examining the relationships between long-term care homes and their local hospitals. Revera's internally developed *Pandemic Playbook* is an action report that emerged out of our daily senior leadership emergency response team meetings. The purpose of the playbook was to provide a checklist manifesto to the executive directors of our sites. It was a guide for long-term care home and retirement residence executive directors on what to do when their home went into outbreak, including how to reach out and plan in partnership with their local hospital. By having identified partners who can build strong relationships and clear communication channels, we are now better positioned to remove many of the barriers that originally complicated treatment for our residents. This example points to an important fact: Obviously, we can't make decisions for those outside our own organization, but we can be clear in advocating on behalf of those we serve, our team, and our industry by sharing what we learn and helping others understand the perspectives of other stakeholders in their proper context. Just as we must build relationships with colleagues and customers, in order to be successful in applying learning or in accomplishing the good we seek to achieve, we have to learn to establish trust-based partnerships with government entities, labour unions, and other organizations.

*Applying innovation to problem-solving*: A key element for how Revera has applied innovation for problem-solving has often come through partnerships, particularly those among entrepreneurs in whom we have invested. A history of such investment positioned us well to draw on the expertise and innovative approaches developed by others and then pivot our response rapidly when COVID-19 warranted it.

You no doubt saw many examples in your own industry of those businesses that had established cultures that supported adaptation and innovation succeed in the pandemic when so many others failed. Some of those innovative responses became so commonplace during 2020 that more evolved versions of them will be with us permanently, whether that is embracing the use of video conferencing to sustain productivity for remote workers or the use of contactless technologies. At Revera, among the toughest things we faced during the COVID-19 lockdown of our residential and long-term homes were the depression and anxiety experienced by many of our residents. Residents, rightfully, felt isolated and missed their families. In order to maximize our residents' happiness and protect their mental health, we had to adapt quickly. This meant assisting many residents with learning how to use remote video access and other means to maintain contact with loved ones, increasing team member direct communication with families, adapting physical facilities to accommodate socially distanced outdoor visits, creating testing access for our team members, and changing our staffing patterns to minimize movement between resident homes, among other measures. Because Revera has adopted innovation strategies and actively sought out team member contributions to problem-solving as part of our larger workplace culture, we were able to implement adaptations as evolving circumstances warranted while minimizing the impact on our residents' mental and physical health. Those residents, like people everywhere, demonstrated every range of response to the demands of adaptation, from those who stoically accepted unpredictable circumstances with grace to those, particularly residents suffering from conditions like dementia, who needed extra team member support. Breaking routines can have devastating mental health effects for some of our residents, and our team traditions of offering high "point of touch" care—being the supportive, engaged, compassionate, familiar faces our residents needed in times of stress—became more important than ever. Some adaptations came with high fiscal expenditures. Others taxed our team members, who already work in demanding, stressful environments. Keeping steady to our purpose demanded doing what we already did well in a time when it mattered more than ever. I was extremely proud of our teams for their ability to think on their feet, propose innovative suggestions, and adapt to fluid situations. They consistently did so while respecting our residents' dignity and helping them find fulfilling outlets despite serious constraints. When a pandemic threatened to turn residents' homes into prisons, our teams found ways to sustain their intellectual curiosity, creativity, and sense of purpose by flexing their own imaginative muscles.

*The importance of a cooperative, open culture:* We made the difficult decision to close down our homes to external visitors well before the government began to issue guidance and eventually to mandate lockdowns. That was no easy decision, for we foresaw many of the consequences for our residents and teams. We knew we needed to take measures to protect our residents' safety; doing so is and must always be the default position in this industry. Yet other precautionary measures were often stripped away from us by forces external to the organization. There is an important lesson here for leaders. No entity can force change on its own. This is a fact that can be profoundly frustrating. In ways that are probably familiar in your own industries, Revera must address not only the needs of shareholders, capital partners, team members, and residents, but also the decisions made by government regulators, politicians, media, union officials, and the leadership teams of other healthcare organizations can force our hand in ways that can have monumental and lasting effects.

We experienced the impacts of decisions made without our consultation in profound ways during the pandemic. Consider the example of COVID-19 testing. Early in the pandemic, the Canadian federal government chose to have each province determine the best means to implement COVID-19 testing. Yet the vulnerable elderly living in congregate settings were largely overlooked in those decisions by provincial healthcare systems. Although it was widely understood that long-term care residents faced an extremely high risk of serious complications and death from COVID-19 and had so much to gain from testing, they and the teams who look after them were not prioritized for testing. In all provinces, early in the pandemic the testing strategy utterly failed seniors living in congregate settings. Testing focused on people with symptoms who showed up at hospital emergency departments or the COVID-19 assessment centres that sprang up on hospital grounds. It also took too long to have results turned around to be able to start the process of contact tracing and isolation. But the possibility of sending sick residents from long-term care homes to be tested at these sites was limited by local health authorities, who discouraged the transfer of residents.

As a result, screening of residents and staff became the imperfect substitute. Even after the first outbreaks began to claim lives in long-term care home and retirement residences, resident testing remained totally inadequate. We were all in foreign waters, and I'm in no way trying to place blame, but the reality was that the Revera leadership team was forced to live with decisions made far outside our control. Not until May 31, 2020, did it become mandatory in Ontario for long-term care home and retirement residence staff, as well as essential family caregivers, to be regularly tested—nearly three months after homes had been locked down. And Ontario was the first province to introduce, in mid-June, routine testing for all staff and essential family caregivers in long-term care. By then, however, the worst of the first wave was over.

Long-term care companies throughout Canada were openly attacked by many in the media for not doing more to protect their residents, yet one of the most meaningful pieces of data imaginable—virus testing—was removed as an option. In the absence of such an option, early on Revera made the highly consequential decision to try to protect our residents by separation, locking down our residences and severely disrupting our residents' lives. Had testing been available in those early days, how many lives might it have helped save? How much quicker might we have seen that infections were occurring because of community transmission? Had testing been available for our team members, the deadly consequences of community transmission might have been significantly lessened in our residences. Wide-scale testing, as later segments of the pandemic proved, would have been an efficient tool. It certainly would have proven a financial and logistical difficulty well worth taking on. While the tired adage that hindsight is 20/20 is true, there is also no doubt that the pandemic taught all of us how critical accurate data is to effective decision-making. Timeliness in decisions matters immensely as well. Some of the most important decisions must be made quickly using the best data available in the moment.

This experience with COVID-19 testing also reminds me that we must become better at taking the generalist's position, holding the leadership role of bringing together the expertise of specialists in a purposeful way so that we can do our best to develop a farsighted vision that attempts to foresee potential conflicts and potential consequences but doing so without delay. The better we prepare as best we are able using risk management practices in tabletop exercises, the better we can make productive pivots and reduce harm to our organizations and to the people in them. The pandemic produced numerous examples of how new data, more research, and examination of unintended consequences challenged the decisions in both the public and the private sectors. Some of those challenges made our decisions more difficult because we could not control all the factors within them. That's simply a reality we're never going to change. How we face what we cannot control is another matter. To apply another adage, while it's true that we cannot relive the past, we do have to determine how we will learn from it and apply those lessons to the future.

Not all lessons have such dramatic consequences as those that emerged in the climate created by COVID-19, but this example offers a reminder not only of how we must adapt to circumstances beyond our control but also that we must do so in environments that are undergoing continuous change. We would go on to see frequent policy shifts regarding testing, mask mandates, lockdowns, and many other realities of an evolving pandemic response. Sometimes we were out ahead of provincial or federal officials, and sometimes we had no choice but to work within the regulations they put in place, but we consistently reacted to circumstances—some within our control, most out of it—as quickly as possible while trying to keep our focus on the impacts we could best predict, watchful for those we could not, and always determined to protect the lives of our residents while maintaining their dignity and comfort to the very best of our ability. This is especially relevant as we continue to surf through the multiple COVID-19 waves and variants into what will eventually become a societal endemic.

# Human Resiliency in the Face of Change

The focus of our mission is always readily apparent in our sector, pandemic or no. The truth of that reality will only become a greater point of emphasis in an age of shifting demographics. The sector is currently home to more than 425,000 seniors at 5,800 sites across Canada, a number poised to rise substantially as the country's older population is expected to increase by nearly 70 percent over the next two decades. As COVID-19 so ruthlessly demonstrated, the need for change—not least to shore up public confidence in long-term care—has never been more urgent. To meet such rising demand will require adaptable businesses focused on the human quotient of their central mission. It will also require a larger surrounding culture that places the highest value on how it cares for its elders.

I routinely feel blessed that my position at Revera regularly allows me to interact with extraordinary team members and inspiring residents. One of the hardest personal impacts of COVID-19 for me was that safety measures required to protect our residents meant I could not visit them in their homes. Similarly, too often my days felt socially and emotionally impoverished because my interaction with team members had to take place via video screens, phone calls, and emails. Outside of those team members who work on the front lines, our Revera family, like yours, had to learn to celebrate the lives of our residents at a distance. In normal times, the people factor of the work we do is routinely present in conversations, handshakes, and hugs. You don't have to venture far—listening to a resident's story about their current dynamics and their passions, viewing a piece of their artwork or craftwork that displays a lifetime of practiced expertise, sharing a conversation about a topic of mutual passion—to be reminded about our purpose.

What those outside this sector probably don't realize is that because we share our residents' lives at or near the end of those lives, we not only come to know them with great intimacy but also have the opportunity to learn from their wisdom. The benefits of congregate living allow residents to reduce the things in their lives that are stressful or that sap their energy and allow them to spend more time and energy on things they find meaningful, uplifting, and creative. Because they are in an environment that stimulates these passions, the senior sector is the perfect place to learn something new each day, and the bonds our team members forge with our residents guarantees this is the case. Our teams come to know our residents as individuals. This people-centred, purpose-driven nature of our work is captured perfectly through a COVID-19 lens in Clare Hildebrandt's description accompanying her painting titled *Death Unacknowledged*:

In long-term care, our residents are like family. We often know them for years. When a resident is nearing the end of their life, it is not uncommon for a parade of staff to visit (even on their days off), connect, and share stories of the resident with their families as they sit with them in their final moments. While death is inevitable, the lives of our residents are celebrated. In the outbreak, our staff stepped in to support residents as they passed if families were unable to be there and held up iPhones to support families in connecting with last words in a new virtual world. Necessary isolation measures took away the ability to gather and to celebrate the lives that our residents lived with honour marches and funerals limited.

> Still, we celebrate the stories of our residents and their families through this horrendous year.[2]

Your business may not create this sort of intimacy with those you serve or make you familiar with the proximity of death, but recognizing that ultimately you serve people can keep your enterprise on mission. Where do you find purpose among the daily demands of leading a business? It is expressed in the energy within our facilities, the collaborative spirit of our teams, and the connection and loyalty voiced by our clients and customers. When we face difficult decisions, we gain value when we find innovative ways to walk the floor, talk with

**Where do you find purpose among the daily demands of leading a business? It is expressed in the energy within our facilities, the collaborative spirit of our teams, and the connection and loyalty voiced by our clients and customers.**

our colleagues about what excites and drives them in their work, and listen to those who turn to us and trust us with their business. Taking such time will help bring irreplaceable perspective and retain the human element in our leadership that keeps us on mission.

---

2   Visit TomWellner.com to view the images by Clare Hildebrandt described in this chapter.

# PART 1

# An Insatiable Mind: Leveraging Courageous Curiosity to Foster Ingenuity

# CHAPTER 2

# Say Hello: Discovering the Entrepreneurial Path

I don't know if it is possible for someone to be born an entrepreneurial-minded businessperson or if it is a learned orientation. What I do know is that I was fortunate enough to be born into a great environment for learning about the entrepreneurial spirit. Both sides of my family, going back generations, were focused on building meaningful enterprises that served people's needs and employed people. They were rewarded for their hard work not only with financial success but also with the neighbourly pride of knowing that they had contributed to bettering the whole community. My family has a history on Prince Edward Island (PEI) that is inextricably linked to the place. When my mum's side of the family first arrived from Scotland in the early 1900s, they developed a boat-building business, they owned the general store, and they owned the Fortune Bay fish cannery, shipping lobsters up and down the East Coast. They also loaned money to support other people in their business endeavors. Eventually they owned numerous businesses. In the 1940s and 1950s, when silver foxes were valuable, they developed a silver fox farm to serve a market need. In the 1960s, they owned the local car dealership—Fair Isle Ford. Such businesses are examples of how they responded to market needs long before doing so was a lecture topic in MBA programs. Through hard work and an ability to spot trends, they understood the nature of a community's constantly evolving business needs. Early on they realized that businesses have a life span and that you have to become adept at adaptation if you are to thrive. You change with the times or you are passed by.

These were the people who taught me to be kind, respectful, compassionate, resourceful, curious, and reflective. I've been surrounded by great role models, including many current and former colleagues, who helped me develop values I try steadfastly to live by and that allow me to continue to grow and strive to stay relevant. At their core are simple principles grounded in an ethic of hard work and an optimistic attitude.

I was also lucky enough to grow up in a loving family and a caring community. Such a childhood anchored me in simple values. I was taught to have genuine respect for others, to think for myself, and to see opportunity anywhere I might turn. I had the good fortune to grow up on PEI, Canada's smallest province, a place where the sense of community hasn't changed a lot over time. It's a place filled with people who work hard and care for those around them. The kinds of principles I learned growing up on PEI guide many of the business ideas you will find in this book. Those ideas don't just represent words to me. They represent the actions I expect of myself and others based on these values that were embedded in me from a young age.

My grandfather, Grampie Johnston, with whom I was quite close, helped establish my principles. Spending time with him, I watched and learned by witnessing how he interacted with others or how he engaged what was an ingenious, spirited mind. He had a knack for seeing opportunity. As the old adage goes, the only thing constant is change. My grandfather was smart enough to foresee the eventual decline in the fishing industry and sold the cannery to a much larger regional operator while it still had substantial value. He then invested in car dealerships, forging a deal with Ford in the 1950s and 1960s when they were in their heyday. He even foresaw that little Charlottetown in PEI would inevitably grow and would one day need a belt road around it, so he bought up land in the places such a road might likely be established. He'd predicted such a need decades before it became a reality. We should all learn from his example because good businesses always think in terms of being relevant in the now, in the near future, and in the long term. Without such vision, sustained growth is impossible.

When I was young, my grandfather had reached an age when he was still engaged and active, but he always had time for me. Among our many activities together was fly-fishing, and from fishing I learned patience, which is a critical trait for any business leader. I learned to adapt to the weather, water, and insect conditions, which I can now see applicable in the business world, for you have to be able to adapt your business to the times and be able to adjust things as you go. I continue to place a premium on flexibility. Philosophically, I am a builder by nature, a builder in the way my grandfather was in his ability to see need and find opportunity and then develop the enterprise that served it. My grandfather was also a tinkerer. He wanted to know how thing work. Like my grandfather, I enjoy complexity and want to know how processes work. We also shared a desire to know how people work as well—what motivates and inspires them, what they find fulfilling.

And just as Grampie had a penchant for building people-oriented businesses, he and all the rest of my family saw the value of learning, both in formal education and by possessing naturally inquisitive minds. Grampie had a brother and two sisters. Quite unusual for the 1930s, both of his sisters went away to business college, one in Boston and the other in New Brunswick. Both my grandfather and my great-uncle Sam also attended college at Mount Allison University, all four acting on the family's Scottish ancestral value placed on education and defying the norm of the times when few Canadians had the opportunity to achieve a college degree. My great-aunts continued to defy conventions, and their examples engrained in me a vision of educated and independent women excelling in business. Aunt Ollie worked for insurance companies in Boston, and Aunt Bea ran the general store.

My mum shares the mindset demonstrated by her aunts and was central in my own education, encouraging me in her belief that people could attain independence and personal fulfillment if they remained open to learning in creative ways. Like my grandfather, she encouraged me to think for myself and to not take things at face value. These are approaches to thinking that I continue to try to apply. I have found that a good leader has to be intrigued by a wide array of subjects. On the one hand, you never know when you'll find inspiration for an innovative idea from the most unlikely source. On the other hand, if you can't understand the shifting sands of larger cultural and commerce patterns, you risk confusing the organization that you are meant to lead. Without people in my life like my mum, my grandad, and the whole of my extended family, I don't know that I would have ever seen the potential applications of such values.

Such entrepreneurial thinking was equally common on my father's side of the family. The Wellners also were businesspeople. My great-grandfather William Wright Wellner started a jewelry store in the mid-1800s and was a property owner who built up a significant number of rental properties in Charlottetown. My uncle Lloyd and my father also had a marine construction company that built bridges and wharves and serviced harbours around PEI. Dad had his own small business that was a specialized procurement company. Like my mother's family, my dad and his brother and their ancestors modeled hard work, dedication, original thinking, and an ability to see and seize opportunity.

These are the people and places that have grounded me and that have nurtured a curious mind. Let me next share an overview of my professional career as a leader. From there, having had the chance to say hello, I'll develop some of the takeaways that connect my life and my insistence that an insatiable appetite for lifelong learning is a must-have for effective problem-solving.

# Training Ground

My life after graduation from Queen's University started at Eli Lilly, a biopharmaceutical company. After working my way up through a series of sales, marketing, and general management positions with Eli Lilly across multiple geographies and experiences, I was offered an assignment in Lilly's European operations as the executive director of marketing and sales. This was very exciting for a young executive, and I found this role enabled me to work with some seasoned executives across Lilly's European operations and those with whom we did business. We were gearing up to launch a series of new medicines across the EU—ultimately more than seven in four years—so I had the chance to lead the market preparation across each of these therapeutic areas and lead/coach some amazingly talented people. I was based in the UK but travelled constantly to ensure that our operational teams in each EU country had the most up-to-date materials and preparations for the series of launches. We were successful in exceeding most of our launch preparation metrics, and after almost five years, a general management position opened in our German business. This was a lesson in the "sometimes when you least expect it, expect it" vein. I was literally getting on a plane at Heathrow when my boss, Rich Pilnik, called and, much to my surprise, asked me to become the president and general manager of Lilly Deutschland. I was thrilled and scared at the same time. While I had been the youngest person on the European management team when I first joined Lilly European operations and I spoke French functionally, "Ich sprach keine Deutsch"—"I spoke no German." "Ich bin Tom" was about it; however, the German team welcomed me, even though they really did not know what to make of this Canadian they had worked with in marketing over the past few years. It turned out to be a really good fit for the German team and for me. I valued my time in Germany and the many lessons I learned working with my German team and with my colleagues at Lilly.

Even though Lilly Germany had provided an autonomous general management leadership role in a dynamic environment at a large Fortune 100 company, I was getting restless and was faced with an important decision—to stay in a known corporate environment or take a risk and try something new. As a family with young children and an ocean between the people and places we knew best, my wife and I decided it was time to return home to Canada. After a lot of reflection, I knew I wanted to experience the world of running a private equity-backed business. That sort of desire is a big part of my personality, for I like tackling new opportunities that require significant learning curves—such things feed my innate curiosity. That move was realized with my first CEO position at Therapure Biopharma. Prior to my arrival, the original company had been purchased out of receivership and needed redefinition of its mission, vision, and values. As a management team, we undertook an expedition to identify a strategy that would leverage the knowledge, skills, capabilities, and capacity of the people and the assets of the company. Working together we found a way to transform the company by putting the legacy biomanufacturing knowledge and capacity to work to serve clients and encourage the development of unique, innovative products to treat specialized diseases. The transformation challenge was daunting, but I saw it as a chance to learn a part of business I'd not yet experienced. Most of my leadership experiences from this time forward have been those of being brought into companies at times when they are in need of change, and my ability to instill a culture of resilience, agility, innovation, and openness has been a central part of my success.

Once we succeeded in getting Therapure Biopharma established with some client momentum and EBITDA breakeven, I decided it was time to take a break and pursue other opportunities. I next worked for a short period with a family office permanent capital private equity group that wanted some help with a couple of investments. These were small to midsize businesses, but I found the experience working with the team at VRG Capital to be helpful in learning more about the private capital space, and I enjoyed the energy one experiences in engaging with entrepreneurs. Sometimes in life you take a step sideways to take two steps forward, and you just need to be confident and comfortable with the learning experience because it will likely help you or your team sometime in the future.

I knew working in private equity was not necessarily my end goal. I wanted to experience something related but additive to my experience base, so through some networking, I found an interesting opportunity to lead a public company and was recruited into the role of president and CEO of CML Healthcare, a diagnostics business and one of Canada's largest publicly traded healthcare companies. There I worked very closely with the chair and the board to refocus the strategy and execute a cultural transformation. CML's core business was providing essential medical diagnostic and laboratory services that had a true impact on people's lives to diagnose illness or confirm health. This was an exciting space providing diagnostic services that had the ability to guide important medical decisions, literally able to determine a treatment path or highlight an impending unsolvable challenge. I arrived at CML with the specific task of transforming a business that had allowed its core laboratory operations to stagnate in the Canadian market and had chased a deal into the US diagnostic imaging market. The US investment had not gone well, so the board had decided that it was best to retrench. My job was to ensure that the divestment of the US business was completed and a new strategy put in place that focused on rebuilding the core while removing distractions. We started with the rebuilding of the core laboratory, patient care centres, and logistical technology operations. Simultaneously, our growth strategy involved acquiring new and innovative privately sourced laboratory diagnostic tests/businesses.

We developed a fast-moving entrepreneurial culture that enabled us to transform through some active business development events and a series of specialized laboratory acquisitions. Ultimately, we built a somewhat antiquated lab and imaging company into one that was state of the art. Plan A was to continue to refine this focus and to take the company private so that we could complete this journey. We were fortunate to get a compelling inbound offer from a large global private equity group. I discussed this opportunity with my board, and we agreed to run a targeted competitive process to enable shareholders to get maximum value. We worked with our Goldman Sachs advisors and successfully attracted a number of interested bidders but ended up with two bidders who both could look at business strategically beyond the net asset value, which took the initial offers up significantly. In the end, we were able to crystalize a 60 percent premium to our share price, and we agreed to be acquired and merged into LifeLabs, which was owned by Omers–Borealis Infrastructure, a large Canadian pension fund. As part of the transition, I was asked to stay on for a period of time to support the integration of the two complex businesses as co-CEO of LifeLabs.

After closing the transaction and the setup of the merger integration, I started to reflect on what I had learned and to consider what new challenges would allow me to grow. At my urging, the board and shareholders agreed it was best to allow for one CEO to lead the business, so I completed my commitment and was once again a free agent. I had gained insights into institutional pension funds through the LifeLabs/CML experience, and I met with Neil Cunningham, a compelling leader from one of Canada's largest and most respected pension funds that owned a large business in the seniors' care and housing space. What did I know about seniors' care and housing, I pondered? From a more personal standpoint, I found the focus of the company of interest because I knew that my grandparents needed such services, and it wouldn't be long before my parents might be looking for life change. It felt like a potential opportunity to really make a difference and help improve the aging experience. I could leverage my healthcare experience and combine it with other skills I had learned along the way. This was how I was recruited into my present role at Revera.

There I've had the opportunity to work with a board and a management team that was up for creating a culture focused on an innovation agenda. Much like I had back when I had started at Eli Lilly, I found at Revera an organization that lived by a core set of values that aligned with my own. I've worked hard to help foster a culture that is rooted in these values of respect, integrity, compassion, openness, and excellence while having to make some difficult business and people decisions along the way to ensure sustainability and relevance over time, even, as you've seen, during a global pandemic.

# Foster Lifelong Learning

You've seen my willingness to undertake risk and enter new industries and challenging leadership positions. That aspect of my personality formed early on and was firmly supported by both of my parents. Perhaps the first major example that prepared me for the professional career I've outlined came with my desire, at thirteen, to experience life off the island, which was fulfilled when I received a scholarship to attend a small boarding school in New Brunswick. I left PEI and took a boat to the mainland to continue my education at Rothesay Collegiate, now Rothesay Netherwood School. I was a shy kid and was interested in getting off PEI and experiencing the world, not an unusual desire for a kid in a small, faraway province. Still, going away to school wasn't easy. I had to get over homesickness, which hit me hard because I was introverted, but the experience taught me resiliency and methods for overcoming my insecurities. I still remember when my dad took time away from his business to make a special boat trip across the Northumberland Strait to make sure I felt supported as I settled in.

Thirteen is such a formative age, and I trace so many important life lessons to my time at Rothesay and to the people I met during the years I spent there. I got to know the parents of classmates, several of whom operated businesses of a scale that controlled major aspects of the provincial economy, among them the largest developers in Eastern Canada, as well as some of the oldest and most successful family businesses in Canada—families like the Irvings, the McCains, and the Olands. Meeting those families was eye-opening and instructive, particularly for a boy who had grown up in such a small province. It helped me begin to understand the dynamics of how business and influence work and the nature of interconnected trade. More than simply being exposed to those with money, I began to see how money could be put to work and how whole economies could be influenced by those who invested in their communities.

I had a number of teachers who proved inspirational and who helped shape my thinking, but perhaps the greatest influence on my development was one of my hockey coaches, Reg Sinclair. Hockey and other sports had always been a way for the shy kid I was to fit in, build self-confidence, and learn the value of a team. Reg Sinclair was the president of Maritime Beverages, the Pepsi bottler and distributor in Saint John, New Brunswick. He was an extremely respected businessman and influential citizen. It says a lot about Mr. Sinclair that he chose to volunteer his time to coach a group of boys at a boarding school, for he not only had once been the vice president of Pepsi International but also the NHL's top rookie scorer in the 1950–1951 season with the New York Rangers. Despite success in the NHL, Reg wanted to put his McGill University degree to use and left hockey to work for Pepsi for $275 a month. He ascended through the Pepsi company with the speed he had in the NHL. Yet the man I met was humble, a true gentleman, full of wisdom, and a great teacher. He gave generously to the community and was deeply involved in many of its organizations. He'd been wildly successful at everything he'd put his mind to and had lived all over the world. Yet he chose to spend some of his precious time coaching a group of adolescent boys.

His lessons were not lost on me. He helped me understand the importance of giving back. He not only offered valuable advice but also made me believe that I could achieve whatever I set my mind to accomplishing. I came from a family that valued hard work, and Mr. Sinclair set a tremendous example that a strong work ethic could get you places. He was a role model who balanced a successful business with sports and civic leadership, all the while clearly loving life as evidenced by the affection he showed for his wife of more than fifty years, Ronnie. The idea of balance has been a central theme of my adult life, and Mr. Sinclair was a living embodiment of how loving what you do molds you into the kind of successful leader who never loses sight of what you value and where you come from.

My time at Rothesay was formative in ways beyond the amazing people I met there. Rothesay Collegiate was steeped in the old English traditions of boarding schools, interested in challenging its students academically and grooming them to become civic-minded, productive leaders contributing to the larger good of society. I shared those values and still do. I valued the education I received there and used it as a catapult to university. It's those values I hold for education that contributed to my wife and I finding each other, and it has certainly shaped the choices we have made to create the right educational experiences for our children.

I remain deeply committed to lifelong learning, something emphasized at Rothesay. The one thing I never worry about is being bored. In fact, what I've had to learn as a leader is to try to shrink the number of things that I place on people's agendas because I find so many things to be interesting. I think it is vital to learn as much as you can however you can. I find myself learning in every environment—from books, from working with great people, from online sources, and from learning by doing. In virtually every leadership role I have ever taken, I entered terrain where there were aspects of each industry I needed to learn—from the research and development process for creating new pharmaceuticals to understanding the nuances of real estate transactions. In order to learn new things well, you've got to learn from every resource you have at your disposal.

The premium I place on education and lifelong learning has been critical as a leader, not only in continuous self-education but also in making certain we offer programs for our employees to expand their knowledge formally and by ensuring we create environments where learning is supported and reinforced. At Revera, we define our values by three pillars—lead self, lead others, and lead functions. These pillars appear in multiple access modules from in-person classes to online programs, and we coordinate training for those from the front line to our leadership team. We partner with experts to help us design and facilitate our in-house leadership and career development programs, and we fund programs that allow those in leadership positions to attend high-level external educational programs tailored to their responsibilities. We have found that an additional advantage beyond the learning that goes on is that our approaches increase interactions among employees from diverse parts of the company, resulting in better coordination among those with disparate functions and contributing to a more congenial, more team-aware culture.

I see tremendous value in forming a corporate culture where people are encouraged to think in original patterns, examine the status quo aggressively and analytically, and participate in a lively exchange of ideas. One result at Revera is that it is not at all unusual to see employees who start in frontline positions expand their education, participate in our management training programs, and grow into management positions. Of course, providing leaders the tools to excel at their advanced positions requires an opportunity-rich culture and the systematic means of supporting their learning.

Trying to meet the learning needs of a diverse organization is demanding. It starts by seeing value in education. The presence of a distributed network in businesses like CML and Revera, combined with a workforce that has English as a second language needs, has to be highly sensitive and respectful to enable learning to happen and value to be created. That requires fostering a climate where teams can find mentors and teachers throughout the organization. It may be seen as cliché, but I really do believe you can learn something from everyone. Such a belief was cemented in me early on. I was one of those young lads who scratched an entrepreneurial itch from an early age. When I was eight, I had a lawnmowing business serving eight to ten neighbours. While mowing neighbourhood lawns, I learned that different customers had different expectations; some were kind to a budding entrepreneur, some cantankerous, some paid readily (some even tipped well), and with some I had to learn the delicate nature of collection services, deferred payments, and even write-offs. In anything you do, if you are open to learning, opportunities abound.

I was reminded of the critical importance of learning again and again while in the midst of the COVID-19 pandemic. In times of crisis, it's easy for some to fall into despair. But in reality, such times are when learning matters the most. One sustained focus I held throughout the pandemic was to make certain we were ready for the future, which included being ready for the next crisis. Within weeks we'd developed at least twenty different learning areas, including things like learning the importance of centralizing communications with our chief medical officer and making her the source of authority. We improved channels for communication with the residents' family members. We learned how to improve our team members' flexibility and how to streamline our procurement process. Most importantly, we found ways to capture what we had learned in an executable format, providing us a resource for our executive directors to lead their responses.

Resources can take lots of forms if you are willing to learn. You first have to be willing to ask questions. If you are, there are experienced mentors ready to lend a hand. This is as true for the ten-year-old on their first newspaper delivery route as it is for when they become a leader in a major organization. I have little doubt that my ability to lead our teams as they faced the epicentre of the historic challenge brought on by COVID-19 was due, in large part, to the learnings and experiences that

> **Leading always requires, even more visibly so in times of great change, a desire to learn, reflect, and improve.**

have been central to my personal and my professional life. Leading always requires, even more visibly so in times of great change, a desire to learn, reflect, and improve.

## Valuing Experience on the Way Up

I've had great mentors all my life, from people like Reg Sinclair to Les Merriam, the experienced salesperson I was partnered with by my first sales manager, Rocky Gualtieri, to shadow at Eli Lilly. I'd learned a great deal from the Lilly sales training programs in our initial development school, but working with Les, I learned numerous field applications for how he managed his sales territory and how he interacted with clients. I learned practical approaches. Every time Les entered a new town, he would go to the pharmacy and ask what products were moving and which ones were not, which physicians were prescribing our products, and what kind of customer feedback pharmacists received. Much of this information is available to salespeople today through automated data collection, although I'd still argue there is a place for talking to the people who work directly with a product or service to find additional insights the data might not reveal.

My belief in the value of mentorship has led me to implement mentoring programs within the various organizations I've led. I believe there's no more important learning opportunity. I find that mentoring is always a two-way street, and I learn as much or more from those I mentor as they may glean from me. Whether it is through mentorship programs or other means, I try to have mechanisms in place for gaining candid, honest insights into our organization from people at every level. Having personal relationships with people throughout our organization matters. At Revera, we've got more than nineteen thousand employees in English Canada alone, so I can't sit down with all of them, but I most certainly watch and listen for insight from every level every chance I get.

Some may view the insights of frontline workers as irrelevant, but such a viewpoint negatively impacts the core culture of an organization. At Revera, where business is centred on serving people in their homes, the frontline worker is quite literally the face, and the hands, of our company. Our residents interact daily with waiters and housekeepers, caregivers and activities team members. As for backroom site support operations, our residents rarely know they exist unless some process is broken in a way that impacts them directly. In this way, any organization is similar to architecture, for typically the only time we pay attention to the structure that holds a building together is when it fails. Instead, we're aware of surfaces—attractive, inviting, functional finishes. But just as pleasing architecture can prove comforting or inspiring, it doesn't have value unless the structure itself is also solid, safe, and functional. Service businesses work the same way, needing strong employee and system infrastructure to support, mostly invisibly, a core of frontline personnel who provide the service and attention that make the customer feel special.

It's easier to remember the importance of frontline workers when you remember what it is like to be one. In my case, because I needed to help pay for boarding school and university, every summer when I came home, I went to work. At fourteen, I landed a job with a locally owned hotel chain on PEI called Rodd Royalty Resorts. I started out washing dishes and helping in the kitchen. Then I was promoted to a short-order cook. Eventually, I was asked to split my time between the kitchen and shifts covering the front desk as a night clerk. From the front desk, I learned a great deal about how a hotel runs. The front desk not only becomes the point of contact for the customer but also its personnel interact constantly with housekeepers, bellhops, repair personnel, and restaurant employees. I began to learn about accounting and bookkeeping and to work with the registration system and management. Obviously, at fourteen, I didn't have any experience with anything, but through closely watching and working with others, whether they were chefs or waiters or clerks, I learned. Because of the nature of how my mind works, I began to see efficiencies and needed coordination between departments.

I also learned the power of having clear expectations for how employees interact with guests, what I like to label the value of learning to look people in the eye and say hello. In the hospitality business, *hospitality* is everything. In hotels, customers are called guests for a reason. Hotel guests are typically vacationers taking a well-needed respite from their demanding lives or businesspeople exhausted from long days of meetings and inconvenient travel. They appreciate a friendly face and some creature comfort. But the truth is, all businesses share aspects of the hospitality industry. Putting others first, whether they are clients or colleagues, creates an environment where people want to be. Greeting someone with a smile and a simple hello is more than good customer service. When doing so is genuine, we create a connection with that other person, and we show them that they have value. It's such a simple starting point but behind it is an attitude that is so much bigger.

Such lessons in customer engagement were reinforced and formalized when I moved on from Rodd Royalty Resorts to a summer job at the local Hilton-owned property. There I began to understand how the expectations of customer service and operational processes could be scaled across a vast corporation. It reinforced the need for training to standards and also the importance of inspections/controls over quality so that a consistent differentiated experience was created for the customer. There I took on even more roles, including the intensive customer contact view of serving as a waiter. In this role, I quickly recognized that my tips were directly tied to my ability to make a guest's experience feel special and memorable. Maybe everyone should be required to work for a time as a waiter or in some other direct service role, for there are lessons to be learned that have application for every industry. It truly made me appreciate the need to be humble, and I learned the multitasking required to keep people's specific preferences in mind. I held a number of service positions throughout my years in college—at Hilton, in campus positions at university, and at the campus pub—and far more than simply providing a way to pay for my education, I also received an education every day. That's an attitude we should carry into everything we do, for lessons await us if we possess minds willing to learn them.

These are the sorts of lessons we can learn only by having our feet on the ground and from hanging around with those with experience. Formal education matters a great deal, but we've also got to get out and work, preferably from the bottom up so that we can really understand the fundamental workings of a business. One gentleman who cemented such lessons in me was Bill Ringo. I met Bill when I was a young manager early in my career at Eli Lilly and he was the president of Lilly Canada. One of the first things I learned from Bill was his ability to project calmness into a room through his measured response and his clarity of voice. His manner of communicating instilled confidence in our team no matter what we were dealing with. When we learned about the early expiration of the Prozac patent in Canada, which was going to be potentially devastating for our overall business, I was the head of the strategic planning unit. We were tasked with exploring our alternatives. Bill was able to calm people but guide them to focus on solutions. This learning was highly valuable during my time at Lilly Germany when we learned one Friday about a week into my tenure that our Zyprexa patent was at risk of early expiry, which would have been devastating to our German business. I remembered how Bill projected calm and a source of clarity. Recalling his demeanor and focus on the end objective helped me lead our work through an orderly set of approaches to the identification and management of the risks required to develop our strategy. At Lilly, we succeeded by creating more flexibility in our organization, assembling a strong intellectual property position, and adjusting some commercial arrangements.

I credit much of my leadership style to the humble, meaningful work of my youth and childhood and to the eclectic variety of companies in which I've held leadership positions. A reflective look backwards across my career probably says something about my personality and points to a recognition that constantly changing times demand flexible, nimble organizations. Anyone who knows me will attest that I'm driven, but my drive is fueled equally by a desire to grow professionally and by a hunger to learn new things.

> **It is incremental improvement that ultimately defines the direction of a company, but that improvement must be constant, and it must be guided by mission and purpose.**

All the stages of my career have taught me to believe it is possible to satisfy the expectations of shareholders while improving the lives of customers and team members. As I have tried to achieve this balance, I've learned a good deal about who I am and who I am not. I am not a CEO who is controlling and entrenched in an inflexible vision who repeats the same playbook for each opportunity. I don't dictate. Rather, in addition to ensuring an overarching strategy, I have acted on a belief that it is the little things that matter most. It is incremental improvement that ultimately defines the direction of a company, but that improvement must be constant, and it must be guided by mission and purpose. I try to listen to those around me and make collaborative decisions whenever possible. I enjoy challenging myself and those around me to think in new ways and explore new approaches. I believe being courageously curious jumpstarts the path to innovation. In my experience, I believe people are motivated by work that is engaging. People need to feel proud of what they do. When we pursue new solutions to problems—some of them as old as our industries, some never seen before—the journey is more satisfying and arriving at the destination is more meaningful to our team. I am firmly convinced that we must be willing to innovate if we are going to be able to arrive at our desired destinations at all. Without an ability to adapt, a business fades into the past.

When I use the phrase "say hello," it's shorthand for a mindset about how we approach our work. It's about keeping in mind that people are at the centre of our organizations. Only with such knowledge can we adjust and learn through a practical lens. It is important to get out from behind your computer and spreadsheets and to deeply understand customer needs through observations or other means so that you drop assumptions, understand nuances, and learn what refinements are required. I strive to never miss an opportunity to meet face-to-face with our customers. People are why businesses exist. Sometimes it is possible to learn as much from a complaint as it is from praise, and keeping lessons timely and embedded in reality is tremendously important. It may be less obvious if you are a manufacturer or a market analyst, yet this fact remains as true as it is for hotelkeepers and nurses.

Ultimately, learning in many forms is about staying relevant. You have to be relevant whatever your role in your organization and whatever the stage of your career. That's as true in life as it is in work. Take a moment to reflect on the values you've learned along the course of your life and on the people who helped you get where you are. Then tomorrow, when you arrive at work, your head already overwhelmed with all the demands that are on your plate for the day, stop and say hello to someone you rarely greet. You might just be surprised how your outlook changes and orients your purpose.

# HAVE YOU CREATED A CULTURE THAT SUPPORTS AN ENTREPRENEURIAL SPIRIT?

- Does your organization have a systematic framework for guiding employee education specific to their responsibilities? If so, are such programs led by those with expertise in instructional design?

- Does your organization have a formalized mentoring program in place?

- Does your organization create mechanisms for interaction between team members who work directly with your customers and those who do not have customer-facing responsibilities?

- Does your organization have a means in place to support candid interaction between frontline workers and senior managers?

# Love What You Are Doing: Finding Creativity in Curiosity

As much as we should value the curiosity that drives learning, curiosity needs purpose. Facts may be interesting, research may be rewarding, but if the learning we do is not focused on pragmatic solutions for an identifiable problem, then it is not going to result in any meaningful change or new opportunities. A big part of applying creative thinking is learning how to frame problems and how you view them.

We have to balance the visionary with the practical. Doing so starts by genuinely loving what you are doing.

I often tell people, "If you don't like what you're doing, then you'd probably be wise to try something else." The worst thing that can happen is when a person with a negative orientation is allowed to stay in your culture. As our chief elder officer always says, "Be the change you want to see in the world." I suppose my advice is pretty obvious, but I remain amazed by how many people don't seem to follow it. I love the work I do. I wake up each day, even on the hard days, excited and ready to face new challenges. We spend a huge portion of our lives working, so why not do work that excites us and that we find rewarding, work that makes us want to continue to expand our minds?

I like to surround myself with people who are naturally inquisitive and who display great passion for a common purpose. Throughout the healthcare sector, there's no shortage of people who love what they do. To love what is asked of us in our industry first requires a boatload of empathy. Throughout my career, I have encountered people who display amazing dedication to their work and passion for their mission. Every day at Revera, I witness employees who view serving the needs of seniors as something more like a calling than a job.

I was reminded of this call to service in a profound way as I watched frontline workers care for our residents in the scary, never-before-encountered early weeks of the COVID-19 pandemic. Their devotion to the people they helped was conveyed expertly in the images and words of Clare Hildebrandt's *The COVID-19 Series* that I shared in the first chapter. Hildebrandt, an executive director of one of our long-term care homes in Alberta, echoes the empathy expressed and embodied in Wendy Gilmour, Revera's senior vice president of long-term care, and Mary Brazier, Revera's vice president of clinical care. The fabric of what these leaders are made of as humans is woven from their calling to serve others. Wendy's biggest challenge during COVID-19 was not being able to hug people as frequently as she normally does. When a company has leaders who keep their sights set firmly on mission, their vision radiates throughout the organization. When team members see leaders who display such dedication to their common mission, they embrace it. The same is true when they witness leaders who demonstrate the curiosity to learn and to apply those learnings.

Not every industry can save lives or make people healthier or happier, but they all have an impact on the lives of those who buy their products or use their services, and they all have a mission that drives the company forward. Whenever there is a more direct relationship between customer/patient/client and employee, that awareness of mission is central. I saw this in the scientists at Eli Lilly, who, although they rarely had the opportunity to interact directly with those who relied on medications they had synthesized, never lost awareness of how those lives had been changed by their usage. It drove them to continuous innovation in the discovery of new medicines.

I've been lucky enough to work with devoted people like Wendy, Clare, and Mary throughout my career. At Eli Lilly, I worked with scientists who were at the heart of our research and development teams. They were not as motivated by monetary compensation as they were by the desire to make a difference in people's lives. They were driven to find cures for life-threatening and debilitating diseases and rewarded by the intellectual stimulation they experienced in the pursuit of their work. I found their commitment humbling. But I was also keenly aware that their passion and sense of purpose made our company better, and the dedication they showed was often transparent to our customers. Many of those customers depended on the medicines we developed for their lives. Both factors made Eli Lilly a place where people wanted to work. Their drive greatly helped our retention of the best talent and made recruiting so much easier. This is a two-way street: Great people are essential to change an organization's culture, and a great culture allows you to attract the best people. An important element of an effective culture is keeping our shared purpose consistently visible and by doing all we can to ensure that purpose is revealed in the substantive actions the organization takes.

In my experience, that kind of commitment typically translates into team members who look around them, examine the products and processes they use, focus on their client needs, and quickly recognize opportunities for improvements. Whether it is a frontline worker who sees a way to improve a resident's quality of life or an executive who sees a way to scale that improvement across the enterprise, this is creative thinking in action. As leaders, applying this style of thinking starts by placing ourselves in the shoes of our customers and teams. When we encounter employees who think in original patterns and look to implement innovative solutions, we need to reward their imaginative thinking and dedication to improvement.

Even in challenging circumstances, if there is ever external pressure to stray from our mission, then we're probably also being asked to venture away from our core values. Either departure will jeopardize everything else we do. To avoid that, we have to consider the needs and perspectives of all our stakeholders. I ask how any decision we make impacts the full stakeholder spectrum, and I demand that my executive team does the same: How does this affect our residents? How does it impact our team members? What's the likely outcome for our shareholders, for the families of our residents, for our strategic partners? But even as we weigh such outcomes, if an action will harm the quality of living for our residents, breach their safety, or risk their well-being, it's not an action our organization can afford to take.

# Celebrating Insatiable Curiosity

Taking into account multiple perspectives is, itself, simultaneously an intellectual and a psychological action. It requires a nimble mind to be able to consider multiple viewpoints. We can't be sincere in considering the impacts on diverse groups of people unless we first are curious about others' lives, experiences, and opinions. Taking stakeholders' viewpoints into full account is more than a thought experiment; it also requires an application of empathy that goes far beyond compassion. We have to reach an understanding of what is behind different perspectives

> We can't be sincere in considering the impacts on diverse groups of people unless we first are curious about others' lives, experiences, and opinions.

and realize that those perspectives arise out of very real and complex experiences. There is no value in seeing different perspectives or alternate points of view as good or bad. They're just different.

As a result, decision-making often means that we have to become nimble and creative in our problem-solving. Ultimately, innovation is about identifying better solutions. Better solutions require creative thinking. A starting point for creativity is embracing insatiable curiosity. If you love what you do, you never get tired of learning more about it. And if you are going to excel at what you do, not only is there a lot to learn but also the knowledge base is always expanding. The world doesn't hold still. You can't either. If you don't continue to grow, what you know becomes irrelevant. This isn't to say that new ideas automatically have more value than old ones. Sometimes the old-salt part of what you know comes in handy. There's value in experience, just as there is value in multiple perspectives. We gather knowledge across time, and if we're lucky, we hold on to what we learn as we move forward.

Sometimes learning is forced upon you by shifting market needs or by the emergence of new technology. The curious person has discovered new ways to learn and new applications for that learning. By following their nose, so to speak, they are used to thinking in new ways. As a result, they are better positioned when a changing environment means they have to learn and grow to keep up. Systems change, processes evolve, new generations of workers come at things a bit differently from their predecessors. Our customers change, as do their needs and wants. As markets shift and consumer behaviours change, we've got to be able to adapt. To do that, you have to be willing to learn.

I had a lot to learn when I became CEO of Revera. The demands placed on the senior living industry continue to grow exponentially. Boomers are reaching their senior years and are not planning to retire the same way their parents did. They want a different set of retirement living options. People are living longer. This means that more and more people are living with chronic conditions, some of which are manageable and allow them to live independently in retirement residences. Others need more assistance, and this strains capacity in Canada's long-term care system. Longevity also results in an increase in people living with dementia. There continues to be growing pressure for more assisted living suites and memory care units.

For younger-aged retirees and those in better health, the same demographic shifts also create greater demand for senior residential communities, and now, increasingly, more residents are aging in place and facing needs of additional assistance. With continued growth, both retirement communities and long-term care homes require more team members and differing kinds of physical structures. As an outsider coming into Revera, I saw a business that predominantly viewed itself through the lens of a real estate company. It had a huge portfolio of varied real estate assets, mostly through housing that catered to seniors. That market segment made Revera occupy a space that was far more aligned with the healthcare sector than with the real estate sector. We were providing homes to seniors most certainly, but because of their needs and the growth of an aging demographic, Revera needed to clarify its purpose and diversify through investment. Part of that shift was for the company to see itself as a people-serving business. Personally, this people-centred element of the company, poised to bring so much good into the lives of a generation I so respected, was a major element for why I was attracted to the company in the first place.

By stepping into an entirely new kind of leadership venture, my outsider status helped me see with a good deal of clarity and allowed me to apply my years of experience leading other organizations in new ways. I'd had a passion for healthcare since college and have always believed in the value of service. I've had interests since I was a kid in architecture, public spaces, and community dynamics. I had extensive experience running businesses in the larger healthcare sector, and I had graduated with a degree in life sciences. I'd always worked in regulated businesses and was well accustomed to operating within the dynamics of government oversight and its bureaucratic nature. I had experience with publicly funded businesses and had run a company funded by private equity, and I had experience with US and UK markets, where Revera had holdings. More important than any of my past experiences, I was excited to learn new things. I saw the opportunity to lead a company like Revera through a time of tremendous transformation as an exciting prospect.

I knew almost nothing about real estate aside from personal transactions buying homes for our family. The board chairman at the time of my hire said, "We've got all kinds of people who know real estate. Why don't you bring your perspectives and experience, and we'll give you opportunities to learn?" I had a great team to learn from, but I had to start from scratch, reach out to those who were experts, read books, ask questions, and do anything I had to do to learn as much as I could. Because I am a naturally curious person, I found the learning gratifying.

There's an adage about business that I think is particularly appropriate: What got you here isn't going to get you there. Going into a new thing can be scary and exciting at the same time. Our past experiences give us good foundations of knowledge and they've taught us how to learn. As a result, beyond curiosity, there's another quality you have to bring with you if you are serious about learning: vulnerability. It's difficult for anyone, and maybe more difficult still if you are used to being in leadership positions, to admit what you don't know. But I think that you have to be humble and leave your ego at the door. Admitting that there is much you don't know means acknowledging vulnerability. We've got to change the perception that has long existed in business that showing vulnerability is a weakness. Others not only respond better when we are humble but also will respect our willingness to check our egos and appreciate our honesty. They will be more interested in partnering with us and more likely to see successful ventures as team successes. Displaying vulnerability makes leaders human. People appreciate working with and for those who don't act as if they are superior. When we create an atmosphere where leaders are not afraid to show that they still have things to learn, then the natural consequence is for team members to be willing to learn what they don't know. I'm the sort who is perfectly comfortable if you look me in the eye and tell me, "I don't have an answer for that, but I'm going to go find one and get back to you." Provided you do what you say, I'll trust you. In essence it is about striving to foster an environment that creates a safe space for people to feel confident to express their opinions and suggestions to advance the business.

Being comfortable admitting our vulnerabilities is critical to transforming our enterprises because the very idea of innovation requires a culture that supports risk-taking. That takes another kind of vulnerability as well. Taking risks means we have to be willing to fail and learn. We can't accomplish needed changes by doing only what's safe or what's been tried before.

There's no way to discover solutions if we remain static. To

> **Being comfortable admitting our vulnerabilities is critical to transforming our enterprises because the very idea of innovation requires a culture that supports risk-taking.**

accomplish change, we have to be curious and willing to ask questions. Not only do I feel enriched by the new things I have discovered, but they also tend to lead me toward new strategic partnerships and surround me with people I am better for knowing. Learning leads me toward improving what I provide my customers, and it helps keep work rich and rewarding. When we create organizational cultures that value learning in these ways, they become places where people are excited to come to work each day, and they bond together to solve problems. Curiosity's great, but what we learn from our curiosity needs to be applied in ways that drive the business forward. In fact, one of my own vulnerabilities is that there's simply not enough time in the day to ask all the questions I want answers to, read all the books that interest me, or hold all the conversations possible with those who have particular expertise on a given subject. Sometimes I have to be careful not to generate too many potential paths, as it can create confusion for others.

Maybe you don't get quite as caught up in interesting subjects as I do, but I bet you've experienced learning that is so pleasurable you hardly realize you are growing. It's kind of like forgetting that you are getting exercise when you play a sport that you love. When you love what you do for a living, then the learning comes along as a natural outgrowth of the work. When you recognize that you need a new skill in order to accomplish something you've set out to do, then you buckle down and learn what you need to learn. The 10,000-hour rule is also good to reinforce that repetition and effort are part of the success quotient.

The same is true at the organizational level. Not only do we need to surround ourselves with others who are insatiable in their curiosity to explore new ideas, new markets, new technologies, new products, new applications, and new solutions but also we must strive to create a culture that encourages and supports personal and team growth. We want teams that stretch intellectual muscles. We want employees who leave meetings not only saying, "I'm going to do X, Y, and Z to deliver on what we just decided" but also asking the question, "What's next?" In the companies I have led, when we seek to hire, we want to make certain the individual possesses the skills, knowledge, and capability we need for the position, but we also try to assess their inherent desire to progress beyond their present skill set. It is these types of personalities that allow a corporation to thrive and meet new challenges. What I have found with consistency at all levels of the enterprises I have led is that the calibre of people we hire have little interest working anywhere they aren't asked to meet new demands. There's also tremendous satisfaction in seeing the people you provide opportunity become successful.

If curiosity drives the desire to learn and learning determines the ability to grow, together these forces foster a climate where creativity can thrive. And as the next chapter will explore, the path toward innovation requires the creative ability to think in new patterns.

# HAVE YOU CREATED A CULTURE THAT SUPPORTS INQUISITIVENESS?

- Does your enterprise reward employees for seizing initiative? For expanding their education or completing trainings?

- Do you have mechanisms in place to help employees learn beyond their immediate responsibilities and understand your larger enterprise?

- Do your teams meet to discuss studies, articles, books, or documentaries relevant to your business or to your culture? Do you host guest speakers who present interesting new ideas that have applications for your business?

- Do you seek out consultants who help your employees elevate the power and purpose of their creative and critical thinking approaches?

- Do you set aside designated time in your workday to think? Do you structure time each day to read? Do you assign yourself materials to expand your knowledge of the changing winds of your industry or of business practices?

- Does your enterprise have formal mechanisms for supporting advanced education for your employees? Do you partner with a learning enterprise?

CHAPTER 4

# Buy the Barn:
# Thinking in
# New Ways

In 2012, we bought a barn in Alberta. And no, I had not renounced corporate ambitions to become a dairy farmer. This opportunity came partway through my tenure as the CEO of CML Healthcare, which was a leading provider of laboratory testing services. While CML operated 115 laboratory collection centres and was the largest provider of medical imaging services in Canada, 98 percent of our business was high-volume, routine testing for the public healthcare system in Ontario. Not only was this a classic "you shouldn't keep all your eggs in one basket" situation, if we were to grow, we needed to diversify our revenue stream away from a public payor system that capped our annual revenues. We worked on a strategy to expand into more privately paid diagnostic testing, which was supported by our board. We were interested in expanding our market reach by offering drug and alcohol, genomic, and naturopathic testing. We analyzed different ways to pursue this strategy, and rather than try to build from the ground up using specialized laboratory procedures in which we did not possess expertise, we decided we should acquire a company that already inhabited such a space. This follows a belief I've always had: Do what you do well. Get help for what you don't.

**Do what you do well. Get help for what you don't.**

After scouring the market for laboratories that already had testing capacity, we investigated a small naturopathic testing company based in Calgary, Alberta, named Rocky Mountain Analytical. And, as I discovered upon the first of several due diligence visits, attached to the Rocky Mountain Analytical lab processing facility was a barn. Such an unorthodox setting signaled one of two extremes: the company was a truly organic business, or it was your classic entrepreneurial enterprise—invent, grow fast, focus relentlessly on the product or service driving the start-up, and make do with what you've got—traits we might associate with images of Bill Gates changing the future from a garage.

# Thinking Differently by Changing Patterns

Now let me interrupt my own story and share with you what will seem like a tangent. But I promise, it's entirely related to the ingenuity that's at the centre of innovative thinking. We'll get back to that barn in a second. The tangent: I enjoy sudoku puzzles. I find them relaxing. They appeal to the way my mind operates. They force me to think about what is *not* there. This notion lies at the heart of ingenuity and innovative thinking. In business, there is value in seeing what others can't. To solve a sudoku puzzle, you have to become adept at scanning, and you need to do so in multiple directions. As a leader, if you aren't capable of analyzing markets, trends, business data, and valuations, you aren't going to last long. You've got to be good at deep analytical dives, and you must always be scanning the horizon. But what I like best about sudoku is there's no one right way to solve a puzzle. Of course, there's a right answer, but there are nearly infinite perspectives to look at the puzzle, and any number of systems to arrive at a solution can be effective. When I'm stuck on a hard puzzle, I try an entirely different thinking approach. This is the same approach we take as a team when we get stuck on a problem. We find value in our diverse experiences and ideas, and together we can typically determine that elusive plan D.

# MORE SUDOKU: A MODEL FOR PROBLEM-SOLVING

You don't have to know anything about the history of sudoku in order to complete one of these numerical puzzles. But its history is interesting. It parallels a lot of the paths taken by corporations, and they, like it, probably carry some vestiges of their past forward. In the case of sudoku, the core concept was developed by a Swiss mathematician who was looking for entertainment and found it, where else, but in numbers. Over several centuries as the game evolved, it eventually travelled to the United States and then from there to Japan, where it took on the form we know today. Its history isn't so different from that of a lot of famous companies. Consider Shell Oil, for example, whose iconic shell logo comes from its origins with a London antiquities shop that trafficked in shells from Asia when they were quite popular in interior decorating. It was the expertise in import-export that laid the foundations for the infrastructure to move oil around the world.

What do shells have to do with managing your business, or with sudoku, for that matter? For starters, it points to interconnectedness as well as to the frequent eccentric histories of the concepts we follow and the companies we inherit. Some of that spirit can live on, deep in the fibres that make up your company culture. And some of the problem-solving needed to run a company comes through applying old and multifaceted ideas and approaches that have adapted over time and place.

Bear with me a moment. Take, for an example, an expectation of any puzzle or game—it's going to have rules. So does running your company, for there's not an industry on the planet that's not subject to laws and regulations. Any solution you reach has to adapt to those restrictions. But you may face internal restrictions as well, some carefully put in place, some inherited from a past you have lost sight of, and maybe a few more that are of the "we've always done it that way" variety. If you aren't aware of them, they can be every bit as restrictive as government mandates.

Despite a lot that can tie your hands, enough creativity in thinking can allow you to see that there are numerous ways to solve problems. How did Shell get from selling shells to selling oil? They encountered opportunity through awareness of a global marketplace. As markets shifted, they took what they knew and applied it elsewhere. In sudoku, some approaches to problem-solving are purely mathematical, some come with identifying patterns, and others apply specific scanning methodologies. Each has an equivalent in business—statistical, data-driven approaches, market patterns, and processes and methods for prediction, among others. You have to find the approaches that fit the way that you think. Get stuck? Then work with your team and try something different.

Think in new ways. Consider different perspectives. Consider new approaches. Where does that barn come in? Well, arriving at a medical laboratory testing facility and finding a barn challenges the limits of even the best of imaginative thinking, no matter how open you believe you are to possibilities. Sometimes you can't get caught up in the surfaces of things to really identify value.

Despite the presence of a barn at a medical lab (and there's an important side note here—always thoroughly inspect what you are investing in—remember that puzzle scanning), Rocky Mountain Analytical had done an excellent job of developing its market and had become the largest naturopathic testing lab in Canada, with great connections to its client base and an innovative product/service development capability. The company was founded by a gifted man who was passionate about naturopathy, Dr. George Gillson. Beyond his passion for naturopathy, George had studied the business opportunities that awaited investment and recognized that not only was the public growing exponentially in their interest in naturopathic treatments but also medical schools had embraced curriculum for training more and more naturopathic physicians. George was entrepreneurial by nature and had built an engaged team that had become the thought leaders for their industry, establishing credibility with the naturopathic community. In developing the company, George and his team had established systems that were quite adequate for naturopathic diagnostic testing.

But if CML was to acquire them, given the kind of regulatory environment we were accustomed to, it was clear that we would have to enhance the laboratory systems and increase the data capacity in order to scale the business. It simply wasn't the kind of climate that allowed a more homespun approach. Upon acquisition, we introduced operational excellence and additional quality assurance as well as moved the business from the barn to a shiny validated laboratory space. But in scaling and enhancing the operation, we did not want to harm the many creative things the Rocky Mountain Analytical team did well or dilute their engagement. We needed to help them transform from entrepreneurs to owners. We respected the creativity behind what they had built and the entrepreneurial spirit that had guided them in establishing the business, but to grow the business, we needed a broader network for distribution, a more robust organizational structure, and a stronger infrastructure in our supply chain and for warehousing. Our inspection of the business included far more than analyzing the technical capabilities of the lab. We also had to determine whether we could create an alignment with the people and their vision. We were able to retain George and his team. Eventually, after our merger of CML into the fold of LifeLabs, Rocky Mountain Analytical emerged as a core subsidiary and now offers the signature approach to naturopathy for LifeLabs. What is now a thoroughly modern company, one without barns, started with the creative genius of George Gillson but expanded to the scale it has today by "professionalizing" the business.

There's a good lesson in this acquisition: Great, large-scale businesses must always retain the spirit of entrepreneurship present at their founding. But they can't stop there. Not all genuine entrepreneurs—driven by ideas, a will to experiment, passion, and the raw energy of doing something completely new—make great leaders. Leaders need to retain those qualities and then match them with strategic vision, business acumen, and organizational prowess. One necessary balancing act of the leader is to retain the visionary approach that is common in start-ups with practicality. They need to be nimble while understanding that a business must evolve, plan for the long term, develop consistency across its enterprise, and communicate across a diverse landscape.

A central part of what we associate with entrepreneurs is new thinking. Successful leaders and entrepreneurs see new markets and new consumer demands *before* they emerge. That usually means that new thinking is uncomfortable. It required a good deal of uncomfortable thinking at CML for some to understand that in order to grow, the company had to transition beyond the comfortable, steady dependency on tests paid for by the public sector. It took some uncomfortable thinking to recognize that naturopathy wasn't a temporary phenomenon but a growing arm of healthcare. It even took some uncomfortable thinking to decide to buy a company that included, as part of the sale, a barn in Alberta.

If we can embrace some uncomfortable thinking, we might just discover some ingenious approaches to seizing new opportunities. To act on ingenuity will require innovation, and that's what we will explore when we enter the second part of this book. But first we have to talk about how we communicate our vision.

# HAVE YOU CREATED A CULTURE THAT INSPIRES INGENUITY?

- How do you encourage uncomfortable thinking in your organization?

- Have you created an environment that supports risk-taking?

- In meetings at all levels, do you have a system in place that encourages a specific period for open discussion of new ideas? How do you then move that discussion to specific actions?

- Do you have systems in place to encourage and reward employees to explore new markets, new systems, and new products?

# CHAPTER 5

# Communicate with Clarity: Giving Voice to Collective Values

The best lessons and the newest ideas don't have a lot of value if we can't communicate what we've learned. Communication that demonstrates how an organization is applying past lessons to future actions is required internally and externally in equal measures and with consistent clarity. I know I've had to evolve my understanding of the role communications hold in a business environment. Early in my career, as I moved into new and different responsibilities and certainly once I began managing teams, I had to learn how to produce frequent, proactive, clear communication and to require my teams to follow suit. Among my first experiences, I had to learn how to communicate as the head of sales teams, which seemed relatively straightforward because I'd developed the same skills they had. But of course, that sort of upward movement also meant upward communication with those I now had to inform about the team's activities, as well as communicating the kinds of news salespeople don't always love to hear. As a leader, each step in my career required additional communication to new stakeholders. Eventually I learned how to identify the priorities required with sideways, upward, and downward communications and how to anticipate what different stakeholders knew already and what they needed to know. That's a central principle of achieving clear communication—give those to whom you are communicating what they need to know in terms they can understand and in ways that apply to their interests and needs. I'm still learning, but each new position, each new company, and each new circumstance provided me more communication tools and a better understanding of the centrality of communication in achieving organizational goals.

We risk real peril if we take clear, timely communication for granted. We all tend to think of ourselves as effective communicators, even though that's rarely true. The irony, of course, is that great ideas are forever getting derailed by an inability to communicate them, their place in the business plan, or what is required of others to execute them. Team workflow can grind to a halt because of bickering over miscommunicated information. Even great companies can buckle at the knees when the media get facts wrong or when real crises are mishandled in corporate public messaging. Consider two very different responses from high-profile US companies to the exposure of serious missteps in the public arena.

The first must be acknowledged as far more than a misstep but a true breach of consumer trust made even worse by a terrible leadership communication response. You are likely to remember when, in 2016, the US Consumer Financial Protection Bureau revealed that employees at local Wells Fargo branches responded to senior executive demands for aggressive consumer quotas by creating more than two million fake bank accounts in customers' names without their consent. Ultimately Wells Fargo was fined $185 million for its actions. Their response was a primer in poor communication and awful crisis management. Their early public statements failed to take responsibility and did not offer an apology. In fact, their CEO did not apologize until brought before the US Senate Banking Committee. Wells Fargo leadership blamed, then fired, fifty-three hundred employees. And the CEO sold $61 million in Wells Fargo stock the month before a federal investigation began. Wells Fargo remains in business but still has a long road to recover its reputation.

Wells Fargo not only failed to be proactive in its response to the public but also failed to develop the kind of thoughtful, authentic, direct communication internally that could rebuild trust among its employees and seize the opportunity to create a new, open communication culture. Its leaders' failure to take responsibility or publicly demonstrate changes in policies and procedures to ensure that such practices have been eradicated will mar public trust in the company for years, perhaps longer.

Compare their response to that of Starbucks.

In April 2018, two Black men went to a Philadelphia Starbucks to meet a business associate regarding a potential real estate transaction. They occupied a table while awaiting their associate's arrival before ordering, and one of the men asked to use the restroom. The manager on duty told the man that restrooms were for paying customers only. The man returned to the table. An employee approached their table and asked if they needed anything. They replied that they were waiting for the arrival of their associate. The manager then called 911 and stated that she had two gentlemen in the store who "were refusing to make a purchase or leave." Police arrived, and the manager had the two men wrongfully arrested for trespassing. Because their arrest was filmed on a witness's cell phone, news of the incident spread rapidly and resulted in protests at the store on the following day and a boycott threat. Starbuck's CEO, Kevin Johnson, immediately acknowledged that the incident was spawned by implicit bias and released a statement that included a direct apology to the two men. To employees and customers, he said, "You can and should expect more from us. We will learn from this and be better." He also outlined a list of specific internal measures the company would take to ensure that it was realigned with its core values and mission. Starbucks then took the unprecedented move to close 8,000 stores for an afternoon in order to train 175,000 employees on racial bias and how to make every customer feel like they belong.

**If our leaders really don't reflect our corporate values, we're doomed before we start.**

Not exactly parallel responses. We can learn a lot from both. With the Wells Fargo example, I'd start by suggesting that we ought to live by our values, for that was a crisis of ethics long before it became a communications problem. The Starbucks example offers the reminder that the actions of individuals within an organization reflect the whole of the organization, and from the public's perspective, there's no reason to distinguish one from the other. On the communications front, the two examples couldn't be more instructional either, for their differing responses reflect key communication needs: transparency, proactive thinking, empathy, clarity, and demonstration of concrete actions. In order to accomplish these traits, we first have to demonstrate authentic leadership. If our leaders really don't reflect our corporate values, we're doomed before we start. Everyone will take their cue from authentic leaders, and they'll know the difference. From there, we need to build inclusive communication styles from a bottom-up perspective rather than from a top-down one, and we need to build silo-free platforms to encourage information exchange.

To learn those needs and to see how they fit within the broader whole, I truly have to listen to stakeholders and understand their perspectives. With our teams, one of the things I have to listen for is that their personal goals and the goals for the people they lead are aligned with the overall good. We have to realize that we are all different in how we see the world, and we must use this understanding when we communicate with others. Sometimes that means realizing they hold inherent personal reasons for

**Only by seeing from perspectives different from our own can we begin to see the bigger picture.**

certain perspectives and sometimes they hold "territorial" ones based on the teams for which they work and the emphasis areas that guide their work. It can also mean putting on a different lens, such as being flexible enough to appreciate the lens of the legal review or the lens of the government review. Only by seeing from perspectives different from our own can we begin to see the bigger picture.

Of course, seeing from multiple perspectives can be a hard thing to accomplish. It's even more difficult to get everyone on the same page. Some days, it's difficult just to achieve clarity in my own communications. Sometimes a misstep is of my own making. Other times,

I can't identify why the message that I've been careful to articulate doesn't register. Even in the best-run organizations that place a high value on architecting transparent communications, it can be frustratingly common to have it seem like we're back in high school playing the telephone game. You know what I mean; you walk out of a meeting confident that the whole group has had fruitful discussion that's led to a definitive decision and that everyone involved knows the actions for which they are responsible and the message they are to broadcast, yet within hours you begin to hear mixed messages. To keep that from happening requires commitment, constant revisitation, and purposeful application of the lessons that come from past experiences.

While business school can teach you how valuable clear communication is to your organization, it's not very good at teaching you how to accomplish it. Experience is your best teacher here. Clarity is usually best achieved with transparency. I try to keep this in mind, and I ask it of everyone in the organization. Learning how to achieve transparency starts with intentionality. That includes studying past communication failures and successes and scrutinizing what works. It also means watching the actions and responses of other companies, as was the case with Starbucks and Wells Fargo. It's useful as well to pepper your peers with questions, particularly when you encounter companies you admire that seem to do a good job of creating open communication cultures.

At Revera, I believe we've gotten a lot of things right, yet keeping all parts of the organization communicating toward forward progress has been a real journey. I continue to chip away at it. I'm always fascinated as a leader by how our communications get interpreted by others. Usually, I'm aware when I'm describing an idea or a strategy well and can see the lights coming on among my team. Other days, I can see confusion in people's eyes. It's a constant battle to make yourself clearly understood by each and every individual. I'm often left thinking, "If I can't make myself clear on a single meeting topic and keep everyone on board, how on earth will I succeed in getting people consistent on the big picture issues that define our culture and our mission?" It's an unfortunate reality, but when communicating an organizational mission, you have to repeat it and repeat it. We also need to remember the context of the individual and the culture. Realize that a boot is not always a boot—it is a part of a car in the UK and something you wear on your foot in the US.

Like with all leadership traits, clear communication starts with us. If I don't hold myself to high standards, I can't expect them of others. If I value transparency, I have to demonstrate it. If I want an environment where input from others is valued, then I have to be genuinely open-minded and open-eared. I'm learning to be consistent about asking if others have understood me and then asking them to tell me what they've heard and how they think it impacts their areas of responsibility. You need to provide people with a safe environment to enable them to have confidence to openly share their perspectives with you. You also have to be able to acknowledge by listening closely to how they have interpreted what we are discussing.

If an open communication culture is what we desire, then we have to approach communication in a manner that's consistent with other business functions. This means walking the walk with things like prioritizing selecting communications experts to represent our organization not only in external messages meant for the media or at our sites for our families but also to ensure consistency on critical, company-wide communications. We need to position our communications teams for success by making certain that we follow the standards they set and that their carefully constructed messaging on things like mission statements are applied across all of the organization's platforms. That also means applying the same principles of transparency to our communications as we do in accounting, including auditing past communications so that we can learn when we've been successful in communicating with clarity and when we've fallen short of the mark. Effective communications need to be proactive, and learning from the past helps us accomplish that. Like with all parts of business, communications are constantly evolving. We've got to evolve with the times, technologies, and societal expectations.

Sometimes we need reminders of why our work really matters and why achieving clarity in communication is so central to our missions. I was reminded how true this was when the expert panel we organized to examine Revera's pandemic response included in its final report the following excerpt from a letter sent to a Revera executive by an employee who had been a personal support worker for many years at one of our long-term care homes:

> I was blessed to be with [most] of the people who died. I was able to bring their families in to say goodbye if they wished. I held phones to the resident's ear so they could hear their children's voices sharing their most intimate feelings. I prayed with each one. Many times, I confess, I removed my mask so that they could see my smile when I saw the fear in their eyes to give them a sense of peace, knowing the risk, but feeling it the right thing to do for them in the moment.

The rawness of communications from team members like this one have been important reminders to me about the role they serve in our residents' lives, the intimacy of their work, and, in particular, how human and demanding their jobs are. The pandemic simply put elements of their daily responsibilities into stark relief because the everyday presence of death within the lives we share with residents arrived with such concentrated regularity during the COVID-19 first wave and wore so hard on the team members who remained on the thin front lines, fighting what seemed an unwinnable war. The clarity of this communication is striking. It humbled me. It reminded me of the greater good at the heart of our business. And while the rawness of emotion here is not something we would share externally, it serves as an important reminder that we, like those we serve, are humans—a calculation that never shows up on any balance sheet.

# FOR CEOS: EFFECTIVE COMMUNICATION WITH THE BOARD

The professionalization needed in a board of directors requires excellent and transparent communication skills. Yet the principles for attaining effective communication with board members are not distinct from other communications. The simple truth is that I've become a much better board member and a better CEO than I used to be. The biggest reason is that I've served on a variety of boards and I've gained valuable experience running different kinds of businesses. I've experienced great models and great mentors.

Good communication with your board starts with being fully transparent. You don't want board members feeling surprised. While it's important that you don't mire them in day-to-day operations or emphasize topics that aren't of direct interest to them, they want and deserve to be kept abreast of those things that affect shareholder value, the direction the company is headed, and how current discussion items influence the company's purpose. They need to be among the first to know, and they should feel that they have an important say in key decisions. To do this effectively requires good judgment to get the balance right.

I always arrive at board meetings with three strategic questions, "my dilemmas," to ask for input from board members. I've found this focuses discussion, keeps singular board concerns from spiraling into a deep dive, and helps produce discussion points that will be useful to management. A successful board meeting is not measured by whether we get through our magnificent slide presentations but by whether we've generated discussion in the right areas that confirm or enhance the decision on the key strategic questions the board needs to approve so that we move the business forward.

Perhaps the biggest communications need for board members is to provide context behind a recommendation I am making. It's my job to help them understand how an opportunity fits within the larger strategic plan of the company and how it will impact both its bottom line and its core mission. I also have to personalize the context of a discussion item in a manner such that each member can understand why it is important and how it will affect the company. If I have an eight-member board, I'm never going to get all eight thinking alike, but I can communicate ideas in ways that those who hold differing opinions understand and respect the position I have taken. I have to know board members' personal interests, needs, and thinking styles, and I must make sure I present information in a way that is relatable to them individually.

The clearest communication won't matter if a leader hasn't earned the trust of the board. These are important personal relationships to build, yet central to developing trust is to make it clear that we are consistently acting in the best interests of the company and never playing politics among board members. There's a huge gulf of difference between knowing how to communicate in patterns that create context for an individual board member and pandering to that board member. They've invested in the company because they believe in it, and they have brought me into the CEO position because they believe I am the right person to lead the company. As CEOs, we have to be able to know when we can drive actions and decisions, but we also have to know when to open our ears and realize that we need to heed their guidance. Like all things in life, we have to achieve balance for when we need to drive and when we need our board to pull back the reins.

The only way we will ever build trust is by having mutual respect. No decision gets made by an individual board member, but every member brings valuable perspective and experience. We must organize our approach so that we anticipate their needs and potential questions and make the most compelling business case possible. I take time in advance to understand their perspectives on what I am proposing, and once in the meeting, I attempt to answer their questions before they ask them. Preparation will go a long way toward providing them with the assurance they need, and it will maintain mutual respect. We still have our moments of disagreement or miscommunication, but we have built a culture where we can resolve them with relative ease.

Lastly, I try to engage my board members and to make serving on the board fun. So I ensure they get the chance to meet key innovators, inspiring employees, and satisfied customers. These are ways that allow them to experience what the company does and the difference it makes in people's lives. Board members want to feel involved. We need to help them see what they are part of creating. Get board members *out* of the boardroom and *into* the business.

Board members have a vital role in the business, but they are still humans. Treat them that way. Respect that they have a lot on their plate. Provide them as much information as they wish to have in order to make honest, informed decisions. Sometimes they hear and communicate with clarity, and sometimes they don't. Treat them with the same honest respect and courtesy that you would your customer when you communicate, repeat yourself in a new way when necessary, and link their decisions to the greater good of the company *and* the greater good of all, and they'll be key allies in moving the company forward while acting on its values.

# How Do You Communicate?

- How intentional are you in regularly practicing empathy so that you are positioned to understand perspectives on your business that are different from your own? Do you create mechanisms for others in your company to encounter others' opinions, experiences, and ideas in a nonjudgmental environment?

- What communication tools does your organization use to make certain that its mission and purpose are always central in all team members' minds?

- Does your organization have communications processes in place that help generate consistency of messaging? Who oversees your company's communications? Are they treated as equals to other senior leaders? Do all vital communications flow through their office?

- Do you approach meetings with an agenda that encourages and promotes focused discussion or one that showcases views you already hold?

- Do you create regular opportunities for your board members and leadership teams to see past company initiatives at work or to interact with employees and customers?

- Does your organization audit communications alongside other auditing procedures?

# PART 2

# The Innovation Agenda: Adapting through Invention

# CHAPTER 6

# Empower and Invest: Cultivating the Desire to Innovate

At its heart, innovation is about change. Change is part of human nature. Because people change, the cultures they create change. And because culture changes, the things people want and need change, so markets change. To stay relevant in business, we've always got to be remaking ourselves in order to adapt to these new demands. Just ask Kodak and Blockbuster, Tower Records or Borders Books. Faced with mounting evidence that the core ideas of their business models had changed, they chose to stick with what they had done to be successful in the past. Of those four companies, those that haven't disappeared entirely are now shadows of their former selves.

In 2020, as we experienced varied impacts and recovery due to the presence of COVID-19, we saw sweeping changes in virtually every marketplace. Some services such as online businesses, home delivery, grocery stores, and at-home entertainment all boomed while entire economic sectors went nearly dark. Products we took for granted suddenly became nearly impossible to find, and lifestyles and purchasing habits transformed seemingly overnight. With a shutdown of dine-in restaurants, new pressures were placed on the grocery supply chain, and there was sudden growth in food delivery services and interest in baking, gardening, and canning. We saw a company like Peloton, the in-home, live-streamed exercise platform, which had struggled through a lackluster IPO six months before the pandemic, nearly double its stock value once gyms were closed and people had to find new ways to workout. In my industry, we suddenly had to adjust to a world in which extreme measures were required to protect the health of our residents. Almost instantaneously we had to adapt to the situation with limited and conflicting knowledge early on to take aggressive measures by restricting access to outsiders, initiating screening/testing and tracing, entering into a suddenly ultracompetitive race for personal protective medical equipment, and overhauling many aspects of our team member hiring models. If we weren't capable of making fast decisions and acting on required change, the stakes were, quite literally, life and death.

Not all market change is as dramatic as what we all experienced in the face of a pandemic, but the forces of change are always present. Sometimes the need to transform comes with a tidal wave, sometimes with slow erosion. The forces that drive change may start with the scaled availability of new technologies. Or they may be rooted in

shifting consumer habits. New demands are presented through altera-
tions in global supply chains, human migration to job centres, or
demographic shifts. Change happens.
And when it happens, if we are not
innovative in our problem-solving, we
get left behind. Even if our business
survives, without innovation we lose
out on new opportunities or may only
be prolonging our demise.

> **Change happens.
> And when it
> happens, if we are
> not innovative in
> our problem-solving,
> we get left behind.**

It can be hard to stay ahead of the
pace of change. That's why the first part of this book was devoted
to developing ways to put creative thinking and curiosity to work.
Without cultivating and celebrating those abilities, we can't innovate.
Invention, which is led by creative thinking, is at the heart of innovation. It's also about having the foresight and the understanding of
your industry to see opportunities for adaptation; in reality, most
innovation is found in adapting others' ideas in new ways.

## The Faces of Innovation

Sometimes meaningful innovation can occur in what, at first glance,
seem like unusual ways. That was the case at Revera and our decision
to hire a second CEO. No, it wasn't the case that yours truly wasn't up
to the task of leading Revera and needed help. Rather, the position
emerged as an outgrowth of our philosophy that the best practices for
the entire company were always founded in providing our residents
with living environments that met their needs and lifestyles. The
decision to create this new position occurred within my first year at
Revera. Trying to make certain that we built a culture that reflected
respect for our residents and recognition for the engaged, vibrant

lives they led was one of our core strategies. At the time, Hazel McCallion had recently left her last term as the mayor of Mississauga, where Revera is headquartered, a place forever transformed by her vision and tireless work ethic. Despite her departure from her position as the longest-serving mayor in North America, she wasn't ready to stop working and was happy to allow her celebrity status to continue to ignite change. She was ninety-three years old and could seemingly run circles around nearly everyone. In chatting with the late Bill Davis, the former premier of Ontario and a chairman emeritus of Revera, he suggested that since Hazel no longer had mayoral duties, it could be great to get her involved with the company. I had worked with Mayor McCallion during my time at CML when we developed a large laboratory facility in Mississauga, and I immediately recognized Bill's wisdom—Hazel could be a great spokesperson for Revera since she embodies living your life with purpose no matter what your chronological age. Hazel said she was game for any challenge Revera might throw at her. In 2021, despite our isolation, we found creative ways to celebrate Hazel's one-hundredth birthday. She was one of the first in line to receive the COVID-19 vaccine.

When we first pondered reaching out to Hazel several years earlier, we wondered if she couldn't provide more than a public face for sustained vitality in aging. At Revera, we wanted to develop as many approaches as possible to ensure that the interests and ideas of our residents were represented. One important step was giving residents someone they could turn to as an advocate who had a direct pipeline to our leadership team. As the senior management team considered Hazel's abilities and our needs, we came up with the idea of creating the position of chief elder officer, Revera's other CEO.

Hazel had retired as mayor of Mississauga in 2014 after thirty-six years on the job—thirty-six years of winning over the public. During her terms in office, Mississauga grew from a small collection of towns and villages to one of Canada's largest cities. Hazel is nothing short of a legendary figure throughout Ontario and beyond. All who know Hazel regard her as a force of nature who displays absolute candor, a deep knowledge of political and governmental workings, and a genuine interest in myriad ideas. During her long political career, these qualities had earned her the nickname "Hurricane Hazel," an apt moniker that grew in meaning to me once I started trying to guide her past autograph seekers at airports at five thirty in the morning as we travelled home from a Revera retirement conference in Vancouver. Hazel fulfills the role of chief elder officer in ways that surpass our original vision, and exemplifies Revera's dedication to celebrating the ageless spirit of people. She embodies living life with purpose and continues to approach the world from a point of view predicated on the following: "If you're not satisfied with something, get out there and contribute; don't sit back and moan." Although I'm no match for Hazel, I'm cut from a similar cloth.

We quickly discovered that beyond gaining the advantage of Hazel's celebrity status as a representative of Revera or even as a role model for our core beliefs, she was great at emerging from discussion groups with our residents armed with actionable ideas. Because of her nature and because she is their peer, residents were quick to share insights into their lives. She proved a tremendous asset for how we present Revera to the public and a potent reminder of the knowledge and experience found within our residents.

She was also, no surprise, a great sport, and one of the first we turned to when exploring the benefits of a new technology or other innovation. As a result, Hazel has been a willing one-woman "human trial" for hearing enhancement devices, smart glasses, web-based services, and other programs we have investigated for adoption.

When we first conceived of hiring Hazel, we never imagined having her provide this kind of assistance. This is a valuable learning for any innovation agenda: When you try new things, there will be a lot to learn as you go. You really have to be open; learning is constant. If you're not adaptable, you won't see what's working and what's not, and you won't see opportunity when it presents itself. Another related lesson is that if you are adaptable, the innovative path you start down will lead to intersections offering other innovations and applications. To seize advantage, you've got to be nimble.

When I look at the decision to hire Hazel, it offers several additional important learnings about implementing innovation. Any attempts at innovation must be focused on a problem in need of a solution. Some get caught up in the excitement and novelty associated with innovation and end up applying measures only for the sake of innovation. Real innovation isn't about following trends or doing what seems in vogue.

> **Real innovation isn't about following trends or doing what seems in vogue.**

In fact, most of the famous "innovations" in history are examples of applying a process or a technology from one sector to a new one. In this case, hiring Hazel McCallion might not seem to the outsider as innovative at all, for as a society we are too quick to dismiss the insights we can gain from our elders. Yet gaining meaningful insights into the experiences of our residents isn't quite as easy as sending out a survey. There are a number of ways Hazel brings vision to our leadership team; being able to put yourselves into the bodies, eyes, and minds of seniors helps guide our decision-making. There are unique perspectives offered by those who interact with our team members, make their homes in the communities we manage, and live within physical bodies undergoing the biological processes of aging. You may direct an enterprise far afield from senior living, but I assure you that there are numerous stakeholders, certainly among your teams and among your customers, who have perspectives on your business you can't understand (or may not see at all) because you don't share their experiences.

# The Nature of Innovation

Now it's true that we might have had Hazel and several residents experiment with wearing smart glasses to test a technological means at offsetting an aging deficit, but we shouldn't think of innovation as coming only through technological channels. Certainly, I will be sharing learnings I've encountered through implementation of technology, and indeed, I'm a big champion of the kinds of advances and cost savings technology can provide. Too often we try to make antiquated systems work in a modern age with corporations that are of a scale we once thought unimaginable. It's essential to keep up with technology, but it can't fix everything. Another lesson learned through the creation of the position of chief elder officer is the reminder that innovation starts and ends with people, not things. In the senior living sector, if we put technology in place and no one uses it because we failed to test the interface for our demographic, the technology is pointless. The same result is true if we use a great new technological improvement, but it is focused on a minor aspect of our enterprise. When you are learning a new technology, it can seem daunting, but because it is a manufactured thing, ultimately it is two-dimensional. Three-dimensional people are the most complex and unpredictable investment any enterprise makes, but an investment in people can have the highest value of return. Bringing Hazel into this position was not only a literal investment in her but also an investment in a philosophy of living that she embodies, which meant it was an investment in our core values.

That last statement says something important about innovation. The innovative solutions we undertake have to be aligned with and focused on influencing what is central to who we are, how we operate, and what is at the core of our business model and our culture. Because of the sheer scale of many corporations, factoring in the volume of work and the frequent relative isolation of back-office functions, it's easy to lose sight of those customers who are the centrepiece of a business. Successful innovation concentrates on the people and the needs that are at a business's heart. At Revera, that means any change we consider must improve the lives of our residents, their families, or our team members. Such improvement might be direct, like discovering a superior walker or introducing pathway lighting to reduce fall hazards (which, by the way, is a nice example of an existing innovation simply put to work in a new environment, for such lighting has been used on airplanes and in theaters for decades, but in a seniors apartment, it gains new life). Or it can be indirect, like making our people and financial systems cloud based to make them more efficient and easier to use. This last example, something we did undertake corporate-wide at Revera through partnering with Workday, not only helped our employees but also created accountabilities and cost savings we redirected to resident living and freed time for frontline teams to interact with residents.

We didn't stop there. Building on what we discovered through Hazel McCallion's role as chief elder officer, our former senior vice president of innovation and strategic partnerships, Trish Barbato, oversaw the formation of an initiative at Revera we termed "Innovators in Aging." This initiative had three essential arms, one of which was creating ways for the residents in our communities to provide feedback on what kinds of resources and services would be the most helpful. One element for providing residents agency was to recruit two innovation ambassadors—Bill Jarvis and Dennis Champ—both residents in Revera communities. Bill and Dennis had the unique skill sets and previous experience to solicit honest responses from residents and the energy to pursue how what they learned—the good, the bad, and the ugly—could be used to guide us to new solutions. One thing we've tried to do is follow Trish Barbato's lead and shift the way we look at problems in the first place. Trish reminds us that when someone approaches us with a problem, we should try to hold back from offering solutions and instead spend more time first exploring the nature of the problem. The deeper exploration of the problem will often unearth insights that can be revealing and help us see the problem in a new light. Doing so expands the possible solutions that become visible.

The five-year Innovators in Aging program sought to approach problems in such a manner, and as a result, was multifaceted. It sought out innovative ideas not only from residents but also from their families and from employees at every level of the company. In a manner parallel to how we approach our residents, we strive to use innovation as a means to empower our teams, particularly those on the front line. When you provide team members agency, there is no shortage of quality ideas. With Innovators in Aging, we wanted to identify practices that either created better engagement with residents, teams, and families or that created work efficiencies. We started by simply cataloging all the ideas, programs, processes, policies, and procedures employed throughout the company that might be considered innovative. A first step for any organization is to learn what's already happening in your business. While we discovered a treasure trove of good ideas worth further investigation, you won't be surprised that nearly all were deeply siloed. Something that was working to the benefit of one residential property had never been shared with another. While it's true that there is local flavour to every property we manage, an attribute we want to sustain because our residential properties are, after all, people's homes, if great ideas are adaptable beyond the specific needs of a given place, there's benefit in scaling those ideas.

In this regard, I've always felt that Starbucks is an excellent model, for they have found a good balance point where they ensure quality control in products and in employee training, and generally they provide their customers with a consistent experience while still allowing for nonuniformity in the design of individual locations, inclusion of favorite local products, and celebration of community involvement. They create consistency at scale while avoiding a sense of omnipresent corporate blandness. This is vital, for you'll never be successful if your company is not authentic, but neither will you be if you can't ensure a consistent experience.

In Revera's research to discover the innovations being practiced across the corporation, we found brilliant solutions originating with nursing directors, HR personnel, chefs, activities directors, physical therapists, and vice presidents. By reaching out, we found purposeful engagement that resonated with our team members. Sorting through the bounty was no small task. Your local coffeehouse might eschew what they see as corporate blasé, but if you operate hundreds or thousands of locations, you have to create the means not only to support all of them but also for your brand to have consistent appeal, messaging, and quality for your customers. Just because a local coffeehouse is hip doesn't mean it's innovative (or necessarily good). And if it is dynamite, the entrepreneur who owns it will face a decision whether they should grow it beyond a one-shop operation.

One result with Innovators in Aging was that we quickly placed parameters on the ideas we wanted to investigate for application. We focused on ideas that improved resident mobility, cognition, or continence, and we considered only ideas that could be rolled out across our entire network. We didn't enter into this commitment to innovation in a token way; we committed to invest up to $20 million as part of our 2015 Five-Year Strategic Plan.

We tried innovations like a reusable sensor for adult undergarments that wirelessly indicates when they need to be changed, which reduces rash irritation and decreases soft tissue infections. We invested in a start-up called Welbi, which is an automated recreation platform, something we turned to after our recreation directors' recognition that we needed more visibility and consistency within our residences. Our recreation managers at Revera Canada love how Welbi enables them to creatively plan, execute, and track recreation programs tailored to the resident. We have invested in BookJane, an app that will allow managers to put out calls for needed shift coverage in a quick and easy fashion and for team members to sign up for shifts when we have scheduling gaps to fill. While these are just some of the ideas that emerged from our corporate dedication to innovation, they offer a helpful illustration of the kinds of ways we found to improve our effectiveness and innovation. A good way to see what we are accomplishing with the Innovators in Aging program is to think of us as creating a marketplace for the entrepreneur. The desire to find creative solutions for an identifiable problem has guided many of the investments we've made.

As we have embarked on some of the innovations applied in this multiyear strategy, there have been plenty of learnings along the way. We've had to retool some approaches, we've successfully exited a couple, and we've implemented one or two where we lost focus at scaling an idea across our network due to other operational priorities. Sometimes we've watched and learned from the larger sector. When implementing new ideas, being first isn't always best. Sometimes you will have more success if you are second and *better* than first and a guinea pig. We all know that when you're entering entirely new terrain, you've got to chart your own course, backtrack, and find your way around obstacles. When you see the possibilities that come with a good idea, it makes sense to complete your due diligence and search out those who have mounted the first expedition into the unknown. This can get you to a successful rollout of a new technology or new process faster and cheaper. Sometimes it just makes sense to be the first vehicle behind the snowplow; it is more efficient to be a fast follower.

One rich example of the complex terrain you must enter when innovating goes back to my time leading CML. We were a large single-site laboratory, doing three hundred thousand tests a day servicing the core needs of the Ontario healthcare system, completing the blood, cytology, histology, and microbiological tests that are requested daily by physicians to enable accurate diagnosis. But we were overwhelmingly focused on blood analysis work— in business terms, our cash cow. We needed to move away from a reliance on the government-funded testing services. To grow, we had to diversify into other kinds of innovative testing along with revamping some of our aging laboratory infrastructure. One example was our microbiology testing, which was significant but was a highly manual process requiring large volumes of human labour and was open to subjectivity. We began to explore the work of a Dutch technology company named Kiestra. Their technology was strong and innovative, but it had been used only in small and midsize hospital settings. The technology included a kind of miniature conveyor belt that automatically sorted all the petri dishes and auto-streaked all the plates, which had photo readers, so they removed human bias. Moreover, the system uploaded and downloaded its findings, removing another huge labour need. This automated process increased our efficiency and improved our quality. But it would be an investment of $10 or $12 million, and we would be the first large-scale lab to use it. This is the nature of risk-taking, for you can't make that size of investment and fail to see a return on it. We had lessons to learn, from calibrating for the volume of tests we completed to managing the amount of data we produced—a reminder that meaningful innovation can take patience and commitment.

This innovation also demanded a lot of change, particularly in retraining the team members to new job functions and building on more advanced skills, which meant a deep cultural change and not just an economic one. Motivated by the excitement of the innovation, a recognition that such technology would put CML at the forefront of change that would ripple through the industry, our team members rallied. The bulk of our CML lab team were well-educated women, and once they saw that our investment included advancing their skills and knowledge, the cutting-edge nature of what we were doing became a source of pride. We had communicated up front with them about the need for change and involved them in the process. When a certain local mayor by the name of Hazel McCallion enthusiastically cut the ribbon to open our revamped facility, these team members felt they were an integral part of a real transformation. In short, we respected them and engaged their expertise to change the business for the better.

We found measurable business results from this transformation, but what was harder to measure yet equally real was the empowerment our team felt.

The payoff for CML was huge. I am mindful of another lesson: There is never a perfect time for change; sometimes you have to bite the bullet. There's never going to be a flawless rollout when you're doing things no one else has ever done before. It's a reminder of the Winston Churchill adage: "Perfection is the enemy of progress." Looking back now, I can see that had we waited, others would have passed us by. You must calculate the best you are able, apply the richest information available, and then inhale a deep breath and take the risk.

If we are going to lead, we will be expected to manage times of transformation, no matter the risk. The world's not going to stop and wait to see if we'll catch up. Strive for excellence, not perfection. And perhaps it's worth remembering that the opposite of innovation is rigidity and irrelevance. Both are certain pathways to obsolescence.

# HAVE YOU CREATED A CULTURE THAT INVESTS IN INNOVATION?

- How aware are you of examples of innovation or entrepreneurial thinking that are already going on in your business? Have you cataloged what innovative practices your team members have quietly put in place?

- Do you incentivize the would-be problem-solvers in your enterprise?

- Do you have a dedicated team focused on introducing innovation into your company?

- Do you have people in place who are experienced at evaluating adoption of new technologies?

- Have you invested in the people who have the skills and expertise to guide your enterprise through change?

# CHAPTER 7

# Do What You Do Best: Identifying Abilities and Leveraging Partnerships

As I shared in the last chapter, as part of the Innovators in Aging program undertaken at Revera, we also invested in several companies using our own balance sheet, which enabled us to engage directly with entrepreneurs. In many other cases, we used investment and collaboration as a means to create strategic partnerships with early mid-stage companies offering products and services that benefited our residents and our business. The first step taken toward any of these partnerships—large or small—was to identify our needs. In order to assess what innovations might best fulfill a need, we first had to determine whether the capacity to solve the problem was something we already possessed.

I subscribe to the belief that you can't invest in innovation unless you already know what you do well. One of the important abilities a leader can bring to a business is to provide comprehensive assessment across the company's breadth and identify its strengths and weaknesses. We also have to think like outsiders. We have to be as objective as possible. When we're putting in twelve- and fourteen-hour days, so everything about our work can feel personal. It simply isn't. We need to step back and put on our analytical caps. I find value in talking to leaders across my organization, spending time accessing the frontline point of view, digging deep into the analytics, and evaluating our enterprise to see where it thrives, where it has capacity to improve, and where we are better off to reach outside for help with services we can't provide with efficiency.

**You can't invest in innovation unless you already know what you do well.**

Let me illustrate what I mean with an example. One of the constant challenges at Revera, like at all high-touch healthcare companies, is managing the complex needs of team members' schedules. I'm proud of our operations and human resources teams at Revera and recognize how extraordinarily well they manage the employee needs of a huge organization, but daily team member scheduling spread across multiple provinces isn't the kind of thing you can coordinate out of the head office.

At Revera, we had invested in a tool that had the potential to offer us greater scheduling flexibility and helped us meet such needs.

Through BookJane, a cloud-based software-as-a-service company that connects care workers, there was a way to handle gaps in team member coverage. BookJane allows employers to efficiently utilize their team members, reduce their costs, and provide better care by giving workers real-time, mobile connectivity to see available shifts and needed coverage. We had been able to get in early to pilot Bookjane, offer their leadership some insights from our own experiences, and help the company grow, all while helping solve what is a problem that directly affects the lives of our residents. That gave us a leg up when the crisis hit. Because people are people, there will always be things like scheduling accommodations to address. No solution is perfect. Even with BookJane we have encountered challenges with gaps in their scheduling module and also with our complex unionized collective bargaining agreements, which got in the way of a full rollout during the pandemic.

But our investment in BookJane is an example of what can be gained by identifying your organization's strengths and vulnerabilities. In this case, we went looking for a partner that had placed all of its energy into solving one problem. This singularity of focus is one of the best things about entrepreneurs and what can make them great investment partners for large, complex organizations. This works well as long as you have the ability to integrate the data and information from the external service into your business enterprise system.

Over the course of my career, I've led organizations in many strategic investments. Let's be honest—they haven't all worked the way I had hoped. But the majority have, and several have proven worthy financial investments while simultaneously offering significant solutions to organizational needs. Many have allowed us expansion in the services we provide. Some have offered cost cutting measures. All the good ones have created greater efficiency and have in turn improved our residents' lives. We spend time getting to know potential partners, not only from a business perspective but also by coming to know their leadership teams and learning about their culture. If they don't share similar cultural values of respect, openness, and focus on mission, they simply don't make for a good fit. If you truly scour the landscape for innovative partners, you will be amazed by the creative solutions you will discover.

Of course, investment is a two-way street. In instances when we invest capital in an innovative partner, their success helps our investment grow, and we provide them important opportunities as well. In Revera's case, partnering with another company offers them unparalleled access to a large network, providing them the ability to test and evaluate their product's impact and gather user feedback in a real-world environment. They are able to tap into our social media and marketing presence, more easily gain access to demonstrate their products at trade shows and conferences, and gain exposure to our strategic partners in business and government. Such partnerships also help new entrepreneurs leverage Revera's operational and financial expertise to help build successful and sustainable business models that can be scaled, seek advisory support from our senior leadership team, and learn from our experience in implementing innovation.

Having used similar approaches in other organizations I have led, I am convinced that, no matter your industry, such opportunities for sound investment are out there. But I'm also convinced that you have to shift your mindset and recognize that forming the right partnerships actually helps your company concentrate its energy on what it already does best. As you consider such approaches, you have to recognize that an organization is like an organism. It has created a human hierarchy and it has been built on personalities and goals over time. An organization, like a person, has a history. People have made decisions that have helped it become the organism it is now, and the personalities of the people who have shaped those decisions have altered the organism too.

Think about the implications of this mindset. On your best days, you are able to objectively evaluate yourself as a leader. You know what you do well, and you know what you need to work on in order to grow. The companies we lead are no different. We have to be able to honestly appraise our organization's abilities. Organizations have to display enough vulnerability—just as individual leaders do—to assess areas of needed improvement.

Because an organization is like an organism, that also means it has a life span. To lengthen that life span, it must adapt and change. Because potential partners have specific expertise, multiple partnerships can make us nimbler. Truly *partnering* with others who bring new strengths, new knowledge, and new assets to our organizations can go far beyond solving immediate problems.

# THE SYMPHONY OF RHYTHM

Nimbleness. Flexibility. Agility. These are all parts of the business orchestra I sometimes reference as the symphony of rhythm. For several years we've heard the vogue term "disruption" employed as a business strategy aimed at gaining a specific market share, but the reality is that there are always going to be externalities that disrupt patterns of business and challenge our carefully developed strategies. Often these disruptions are rooted in new technologies. Sometimes they arrive because of larger economic shifts. Occasionally, what seemed merely a trend gains such traction that it changes demand. And sometimes it is truly seismic, such as what the world experienced with the COVID-19 pandemic. As we all have experienced, such seismic shifts have effects that permanently alter how we all do business.

Yet, even during a seismic shift, the reality is that there are underlying and inevitable cycles at work. What a high-quality strategic plan tries to accomplish is to enter the rhythm present in these natural cycles through careful analysis. I'm not necessarily enamored with the trendsetters and influencers who dominate Instagram feeds and YouTube channels, yet there is something business leaders can relate to in their postings, for they are adept at reading the patterns of culture, lifestyle, and commerce and recognizing opportunities in shifting patterns. Such ability is directly tied to my emphasis on engaging in lifelong learning, for if you are constantly observant and willing to learn, you are better able to recognize cultural and business patterns and understand the context behind changing demands from various vantage points.

Among some of my own learning, I've been particularly fascinated with the books of Yuval Harari, *Sapiens* and its follow-up, *Homo Deus*. When you read this history of the human species and Harari's predictions for the next evolutions of human behaviour, one thing you become extremely aware of is the presence of natural rhythms—daily, weekly, quarterly, yearly rhythms. These partner with cultural cycles and the repercussions that emerge from them. His work reminds us of the presence of cycles in our species, but if we look, we see them in our businesses as well. We are inescapably aware of quarterly rhythms and the hold they have on us for measuring success, hitting targets, closing books, and planning for the immediate future. We have to step beyond the quarter and listen to all the parts of our businesses and to all those they touch. It's about being attuned to the broader patterns swirling around us. In my industry, we not only face the predictable rhythmic cycles of month-end and quarter-end but also must plan for the natural cycles of an older population.

When you're aware of the symphony of rhythm, you understand the distinctions between projects that have to be perfectly planned and those that are more forgiving. You see when you're working on a project where it's important to implement quickly, even if you know it will require changes later versus those where you've only got one shot to get it right. You have learned to take a five-year strategic plan and break it down into lots of measurable achievement points along the way, which not only helps you keep track of your progress but also gives you room to adapt. Now you have to apply those principles by listening for other tones. When you become more adept at listening to the symphony, you are better able to turn to a few jazz elements and improvise.

# Reap the Future by Harvesting the Past

In the last section, I said that organizations are like organisms. Let's extend that idea a bit, for like organisms, this means that organizations have a past. We benefit from knowing the history of our organizations. That knowledge helps us see where it needs to go. Because organizations are formed by people and people have personalities, they form cultures as well.

Culture can be a positive or a negative thing. We need to become aware of the nature of our corporate culture and be intentional in the kind of culture we want to foster. Organizations, quite naturally, take on many of the values of their founders and leaders, and they echo the larger cultures to which they are regularly exposed, whether that is by careful planning or by circumstance. Let me illustrate. When I initially started at Revera in 2014, the budgeting was based on the previous year's earnings plus 2 percent, and the compensation plan was aligned to that mentality. In late 2014, we completed a revised strategic plan, and in early 2015, our board and owners approved a compensation plan aligned with the new strategy. That strategy encouraged our leaders to act like owners and provided an opportunity to participate in an equity-style program. This change of focus helped support people taking a second look at their resourcing levels and business units. We made some tough decisions to divest from nonstrategic business segments, such as our Canadian Home Health Business and our US Specialized Nursing division, along with an orphan retirement

> **We need to become aware of the nature of our corporate culture and be intentional in the kind of culture we want to foster.**

portfolio in Oregon—these were businesses where we did not have a truly differentiated advantage on either our positioning or our go-forward returns. These divisions each had their own set of complexities that were distracting to our core strategic directions.

Every company is different, and we have to start with what we've got, just as we must have a concrete sense of what kind of culture we want to develop. Consider another example I learned early on in my time running CML. It had created a number of legacy dynamics that can probably be traced back to its founder, an extraordinary physician with an exceptionally clear vision of how he wanted his labs to run but a guy who was a bit autocratic in his management style and didn't always allow people room for their own opinion. Early on in my tenure, when I would be visiting with our team at the labs and patient service centres, I would often ask the simple question, "Why are you running that test or process in that particular way?" They tended to answer, "That's how I was told to do it by Dr. Mull and that's how I've done it for fifteen years." Perhaps unwittingly, CML had developed a culture where people had been indoctrinated into a set way of behaving. It's a nice example of how we can understand parts of our organizational mentality by knowing its evolution across its history. Without knowing something about the personality and leadership style of the individual who had founded CML, I couldn't really understand the nature of the organism. Once I understood how its culture had come about, it was then possible to start to reshape the culture into one that encouraged employees to share opinions and think for themselves. Dr. Mull was an inspirational founding figure, but the company he had built was in need of a release to empower the true opportunity within the business and to enable a more dynamic cultural transition.

We should never doubt our ability to shape, knowingly or unwittingly, the culture of the companies we are fortunate to lead. People are used to hierarchical structures. As leaders we must give careful thought to the kinds of organizational values we want to develop, and we must recognize that our own actions and behaviours will set the tone for the whole organization. We need to be conscious of modeling the behaviours we want to see. We're all human, but I guarantee that if we break from the habits and behaviours we ask of others, it will be noticed. Whether we are modeling the habit of active listening, seeking input from colleagues in a meeting, or simply making certain that we greet others as we move about the hallways, no one is going to buy in to cultural expectations if we don't demonstrate that we take such behaviours to heart.

A key extension of demonstrating positive behaviours comes from grooming those traits in others we value. This is most formalized through mentoring. I've already spoken about the value of mentoring when I discussed the importance I place on sharing education and passing along knowledge. But if we are going to cultivate the wisdom of the past, whether that's the history of the company or the previous experiences that have shaped us as leaders, we have to develop structured ways to move that knowledge into the future. Speaking personally, mentoring, whether formal or informal, gives me great satisfaction. There is nothing more rewarding than to see another person grow and rise to meet new challenges. It is energizing to see the excitement of a young person's desire to learn. Even when every moment of our days is booked, we still need to make time to work with those who will be tomorrow's leaders. Not only do we invest in others by doing so but also we quite literally invest in the future of the company.

Whether we are investing in rising leaders within our organizations, investing in another company that can help our business perform better and more efficiently, or acquiring another enterprise that can help us fulfill our mission, we have to undertake an honest and transparent exploration to identify what we do best and where we need help. Then bringing along young, promising talent, turning to experts in narrow but applicable fields, and identifying partnerships that enhance what we already excel at not only will create a true competitive advantage but also will build something lasting and permanent that can continue to grow. When we leverage the best of what our enterprise brings to its team members and customers by expanding an intentional culture through the strengths of others, we create a business that is capable of truly mattering in people's lives.

Of course, the most important lingering question is this: Exactly what sort of culture should we want to create? Answering that will be an important feature of the last major section of the book. Before we get there, let's see what one vital aspect of such a culture—innovation—can look like in action.

# DO YOU KNOW YOUR ORGANIZATION'S STRENGTHS?

- Have you completed a formal assessment of your organization's innovation initiatives, policies, procedures, and past programs?

- Do you have a mechanism in place for employees and customers to offer suggestions, express concerns, and share success stories with those in decision-making positions?

- Have you consulted your company's history and archives to gain a sense of how it came to be and how it has changed over time?

- How do you communicate strategic initiatives to your various stakeholders?

- What period of time does your strategic plan cover? Do you regularly track its progress? Do you have concrete procedures in place for measuring the success of initiatives attached to your strategic vision?

# CHAPTER 8

# Act on Principles: Celebrating the Ageless Spirit through Applied Innovation, a Case Study

In 2014, I was fortunate that the Revera board supported my recommended strategy to transform the company into a major owner, operator, and investor in senior living across Canada, the US, and the UK. What I didn't know was that I was also signing on to a social movement to combat ageism. But I was. Now, a half decade into leading Revera, I see my role in creating social change about how we view aging and how we serve and honour our senior populations as the most important work I do.

Tackling ageism wasn't a part of some grand master plan on my part. I'm a professional CEO, a kind of hired gun who has frequently been tasked with leading organizations through periods of transition. In truth, I didn't know how to pronounce Revera when its board chair first approached me. While I had taken pride in my work trying to improve the cultures and applying more humanism in the other organizations I've led, with Revera, I quickly saw that it offered a mix of the intellectual excitement of tackling new problems I always find exciting combined with the emotional gratification of knowing we could accomplish some fundamental good. The thought of having a positive impact on people's lives was motivating, even inspiring. Moreover, I was enthusiastic, even if I had some trepidation, to learn new things.

I also was intrigued by the challenges I saw inherent in the sector. As baby boomers age and people live longer, I could see both the capacity for sector growth and the need to provide the right kind of growth. In Canada, the combination of people living longer with the population bulge of the baby boom generation means seniors are on track to represent 25 percent of the population by 2050. They made up 15 percent of the population in 2010.[3] These shifts are roughly parallel in the United States and on a slightly faster pace in the United Kingdom. To meet the needs of a sector with this scale of growth required that I do a lot of learning. What I hadn't fully appreciated

3    Jason Clemons and Sasha Parvani, "Canada Must Prepare for Our Aging Population," Fraser Institute, originally appeared in the *Toronto Sun*, November 26, 2017, https://www.fraserinstitute.org/article/canada-must-prepare-for-our-aging-population.

was how much learning I would do by working directly with our residents. The personal growth I experienced in my first year at Revera wasn't limited to learning that would make me a better CEO but also a better person.

I've learned a great deal—about life, about work, about values— by getting to work with and on behalf of people from my parents' and my grandparents' generations. Learning from the residents we serve isn't different from learning from any person of any age who is curious about this complex universe we inhabit and who wants to share the thoughts and realizations that have arisen from that curiosity. Often, they teach me about patience and about finding joy or pleasure in things I might overlook because "I'm so busy." They remind me of the value of living in *this* day rather than obsessing over the future. By sharing stories, memories, and experiences, they teach me to be reflective, to remember where I come from, to be appreciative of the people I have valued across my life. I am mindful of what Monica Schoch-Spana, a medical anthropologist, reminds us: "Older people have been through a lot—the civil rights movement, the women's movement, the Cold War ... They are our culture keepers, full of stories of how you get through major tragedies and upheavals."[4] As a CEO working in environments where everything seems to be regularly undergoing upheaval, I have a lot to learn from those who have been on this journey we call living longer than I. It is apparent that we as humans evolve in repeatable cycles, so learning as much as we can from the past is critical.

There are significant challenges in the senior living sector, some inherent in its complexity, others attached to the challenges that

---

4    Quoted in "Our Pandemic Summer" by Ed Yong, *The Atlantic*, April 14, 2020, https://www.theatlantic.com/health/archive/2020/04/ pandemic-summer-coronavirus-reopening-back-normal/609940/.

come with growth and change as an aging demographic expands, and more still in advocating for the relevance of a population who are regular victims of social prejudice. But with challenges there are also the rewards of successfully leading change and making a difference in people's lives. Increasingly, we'll be feeling the gap between life span and "health span" as it has been appropriately labeled by Ken Dychtwald, a leading gerontologist. People live longer than they did in the not-so-distant past, though not necessarily in good health. At time of writing, there were more than thirty-eight thousand people waiting for long-term care beds in the province of Ontario alone.[5] And our demographics are changing: families with fewer children, families more geographically spread out, and more women becoming primary breadwinners, resulting in less capacity for caregiving by precisely those who have provided the lion's share in the past. All of this changes the demands placed on professional care providers and asks them to improve long-term caregiving services and supports while also trying to prevent medical episodes and improve quality of life. That's our primary obligation: to improve the quality of our residents' lives. How rich, how full, how joyous can their senior years be? Medical research and disease prevention will allow our residents to live longer; now we have to make sure they live happier.

A big part of that happiness is dependent on seniors being treated with the respect they deserve. The vision of humanism is to recognize the inherent value in every life. That means we must help seniors by becoming their advocates against those who practice ageism. By applying the principles that are central to this book about creating workplaces where the best abilities of people are brought

---

5    Nicole Ireland and Natalie Kalata, "As COVID-19 Exposes Long-Term Care Crisis, Efforts Grow to Keep More Seniors at Home," CBC, February 3, 2021, https://www.cbc.ca/news/canada/toronto/covid-ontario-government-home-care-long-term-care-1.5897858.

out through open cultures of collaboration and applying problem-solving through innovation, at Revera, we've been able to focus on enriching seniors' lives while battling social forces that too often want to view them as irrelevant.

Celebrating the ageless spirit and combating ageism is personal to me. Mostly it's personal because in my role at Revera, I've had the opportunity to work alongside so many vibrant, inspiring people who know how to embrace joy wherever it is found and to face adversity with dignity. It's personal because I'm not just a Revera employee; my parents are customers. It's personal because my grandmother, who passed at age ninety-nine during the time I was writing this book, lived her final years in a nursing home called Whisperwood Villa on PEI. The emotional gap I experienced by not being able to be with her in person to comfort her as she passed or to celebrate her life was painful. My grandmother was a woman who had given back to her community all her life. Even in her final years, my grandmother sustained that impulse, knitting more hats and mittens than she knew people to whom she could give them. Her life and now her legacy are reminders to me for why what we do in this industry matters so greatly.

I've been that son who has faced the difficult family decision of helping his parents move far from their provincial home where they'd lived all their lives. I've participated in their transition to an unfamiliar city and the uncertainties they felt in order that they might be closer to their children and in environments where more care was available to them. I've witnessed the comfort they take in a new home where friends are close at hand and where they can make more choices about how they want to spend their day and less time completing the chores that a day requires. As a person with loved ones living in one of our residences, I moved far beyond an understanding of the functional operations involved in senior living to an emotional understanding of the aging process and the best ways senior living can meet its residents' needs.

My experience has allowed me greater empathy and greater understanding. I've held the tough discussions with my parents as they faced realizations about their changing physical needs. I learned to support my dad as he shifted his role to becoming a caregiver as my mum began to show cognitive decline. I've recognized the importance of creating environments where they can live independently, be engaged, be respected, and participate in activities they enjoy. My experience has helped me learn things that even my observational best and my most inquisitive self couldn't know. What I have experienced has a vital equivalent in any business that is customer oriented and particularly those that serve people's most essential needs. Ask yourself, Do you have the ability to see your business from your customer's point of view? Do you make it a practice to do so with each decision that you make?

## TODAY IS TODAY

One of the lessons of working with seniors is an appreciation for what a moment provides. I've known residents who regularly joke, "Well, I checked the paper this morning. I wasn't in the obituaries, so I guess I better go out and make it a great day." The appreciation for what each day brings can be accompanied by the simple realization that they've already lived through a lot. In the age of COVID-19, it wasn't unusual to hear seniors say, "I've lived through a lot worse."

That's a spirit we can bring to business. While we can't ignore problems, we can put them in perspective. I can't tell you how often the thing that I've placed so much emotional energy into, the "problem at work" that has woken me up at night, ends up being a nonissue. Meanwhile, what seemed insignificant can grow into a real challenge.

I think often of my grandfather and his father before him. How many different businesses did they build and sell? How often did they take actions to plan for a business future that was a decade or even a generation away? How often did they remake their businesses as they saw their customers' needs changing? Everything is temporary, as our seniors will readily remind us. We're wise to remember that we should live in the day, enjoy the present, and recognize that new challenges, new problems, and new opportunities will make us get out of bed again tomorrow.

# The Fight against Ageism

My experience at Revera has also forced me to face my own assumptions and denials. The idea of aging as a metaphysical construct is an easy thing to dismiss when you are young. Call it irrelevance, denial, or myopia, but few young people think about their old age. When we are young, we're likely to think about *our* grandparents with fondness in relation to our memories with them while giving very little thought to them in the larger context of their peers or to think about how they see their own lives and roles. As I have gotten older myself and as I watched my parents and grandparents age, I better understand why Bette Davis said, "Old age ain't no place for sissies!" There are hard biological truths that come with aging, realities that can slow one's pace or make one reach out for a bit more help. Yet many elderly people take change in stride, for their experience teaches them that the world is constantly in flux. They recognize that life is a series of stages and that living a fulfilling life is a process of letting in and letting go. They are exposed to death with enough regularity that they see it as an inevitable part of the life cycle. Older people are neither pathetic nor cute, as so much of the popular media seems intent on depicting them. Most see themselves simply as humans reaching another state of their lives that is marked by physiological change, as real, as complex, as individualized, and as expected as puberty.

Yet the rest of us are likely guilty of viewing aging as a slow period of decline. In reality, it is another stage of our lives that can be rich with learning, opportunity, and tremendous happiness. What the residents of Revera's many properties teach me every day is that growing old does not have to diminish your curiosity about a world filled with diverse people and ideas, lower your engagement with others, lessen your desire to contribute to the betterment of others' lives, or remove your ability to participate in activities that bring you joy and that can enrich your life.

Yet that is not the predominant view toward seniors. Unfortunately, most of us are guilty of making assumptions about older people. Have you ever said to a friend when you forgot a colleague's name, "I'm having a senior's moment?" I know I have. When you view an older person playing a musical instrument with dexterity or producing a work of art, do you assume they are an anomaly and suggest that their ability is beyond belief "because they're *old*"? When you see someone walking slowly, do you assume their thinking has slowed too? Do you speak to them more slowly, or more loudly, or in a tone more suited to a child? If we meet an older person confined to a wheelchair and we have a lengthy, stimulating, intellectual conversation with them, do we think of them as an exception to a norm? Do we later tell our friends about the most amazing *old* person we met rather than simply seeing them as an engaged, interesting person? If you've done any of these things, you're practicing ageism.

Not only do we tend to treat older people as if their lives are in decline, in a manner that is parallel with all prejudices, but also we're quick to assume that they possess a uniform experience. It takes very little intellectualism to instead realize that any older person's life experience is as varied and individualized as anyone else's on the planet. Do people age uniformly? Are our genetic makeups identical? Do we suffer the same diseases or die from the same causes? Do we like the same foods? Do we grow up in the same neighbourhoods? One person's ninety is another person's seventy when viewed in terms of mobility, cognition, participation in physical activity, or other factors. An out of shape forty-five-year-old with a chronic disease may be closer to end of life than a healthy seventy-five-year-old who eats a balanced diet and exercises regularly. It's true that because of the biological aging process in which cellular structures change or because of the presence of disease, some elderly people do suffer severe physical or cognitive degradation, but to assume that their individual health is representative of an entire demographic is no different from making prejudicial assumptions about a person because of their race or gender.

The overwhelming barrier to improving the lives of seniors is ageism—stereotyping or discriminating against a person or group because of their age. You're not likely to acknowledge that you have practiced this form of prejudice. You may not even know that you have. That "not knowing" is likely why ageism is by far the most tolerated form of social prejudice. Increasingly around the globe and certainly where I live, in Canada, racism and sexism are rightly called out—swiftly and powerfully. By contrast, ageism is rarely addressed. It needs to be. Changing how we treat older people needs to happen right now. The first *Revera Report on Ageism*[6] conducted by Revera and the International Federation on Ageing found that one in four Canadians admitted to treating someone differently because of their age.

> The overwhelming barrier to improving the lives of seniors is ageism—stereotyping or discriminating against a person or group because of their age.

Much of ageism is subtle. Much of it is not intentional. These facts only make ageism more difficult to root out. Ageism can appear even when driven by pride, such as our common usage of the word "still." Dad's eighty-five and can "still" drive on his own. Mom's ninety and she's "still" as sharp as a tack. Older people have standing in our society only to the degree that they can do what younger people can do. And what happens if they can't? Do they disappear? Some of ageism is fueled by the kind people among us simply trying to be helpful: carrying a bag of groceries, providing an arm to lean on. And some older people may, of course, want or need such assistance. But we shouldn't assume so by default. Unfortunately, by taking away seniors' independence and reducing their choices, we end up doing exactly the wrong thing by acting on assumptions. Our Revera report revealed that more than half of Canadians over the age of seventy-

---

6  *Revera Report on Ageism*, https://ifa.ngo/wp-content/uploads/2013/03/Revera-IFA-Ageism-Report.pdf.

seven say that younger people assume they can't do things for them-selves. Worse, more than a quarter of older adults say that because of their age, younger people make choices for them without asking their preference.[7] We use words like "helpful" and "responsible" to describe how we feel when we make decisions on behalf of seniors. But we need to listen to adults who say they feel "controlled" and "annoyed" when choices are made for them. Ultimately, ageism robs seniors of independence and choice.

We need to be mindful of our actions and our language. Even the word "retire" is fraught with implications that may not be accurate. It suggests that leaving the workforce means we want to disengage. Shouldn't leaving the workforce mean more time to participate in the nonwork activities we value, greater flexibility to pursue our passions, and more availability to extend our commitment to causes that have moved us throughout our lives? "Retire" can suggest that we've reached some magical age when we are now ready to be lavished in luxury and do nothing. Well, if that's your vision of retirement, then go for it. But let's not assume all would want such relaxation or all are financially capable of achieving it. More importantly still, let's not mistake such an association as suggesting that people no longer have something to contribute. It's worth remembering that even the age we associate with retirement (at least in most Western countries)—sixty-five—is an arbitrarily chosen age that came about as a response to economic recession via the formation of governmental social assis-tance programs. There are many who wish to and who should have the opportunity, if they choose it, to continue contributing to the greater good of a society through traditional work past age sixty-five. It takes a long time and a lot of commitment to gain real expertise. Why would we waste its benefits because of arbitrary convention or

---

manufactured societal expectation? Let's not fall into the assumption trap that because someone is older, they are incapable of gaining new knowledge, changing with the times, or embracing new technologies. And who better to mentor the young than someone who has already trod the path the young are taking, someone who has benefited from the wisdom granted by learning from mistakes and who has seen the inevitable ebbs and flows of solutions tried, abandoned, and retried?

But the good thing about ageism is that, unlike most other isms, it isn't engrained with bitterness or hatred. Rather, it's covered with a thin gloss of ignorance, which can often be scrubbed clean by a quick application of awareness. After all, study after study reveals that the older you get, the happier and more optimistic you become—again, disproving another building block of ageism, that our seventies, eighties, and even nineties are spent marking time waiting for the end.[8] Like all forms of prejudice, awareness about its existence is the starting point to ending it. The next comes from listening. Engage with those who are older than you, listen to what they have to say, learn from their experience. Ask questions. Inventory your assumptions and trace their origins, then make a conscious effort not to give into them. If you find yourself making an assumption about an older person, check yourself. And if you witness someone else practicing ageism, call it out. Come to recognize the zest for living many older people express and awash yourself in it. Embrace vibrancy wherever you find it.

In short, be human.

---

8   "Why People Get Happier as They Get Older," *The Economist,*
    December 23, 2016, https://medium.economist.com/
    why-people-get-happier-as-they-get-older-b5e412e471ed.

# Beating Ageism: A Case Study in Innovation

Of course, we will all be old one day. I certainly hope that for myself, and I hope it for you too. Think about how you want to be treated. I'm guessing that how you wish to be treated one day in your future isn't different from how you want to be treated now. Will some of your needs be different? Certainly. This is precisely why, even as we celebrate the aging spirit and we respectfully afford every individual the degree of independence they desire, we must recognize that we have a role to play in aiding such independence. What can we do to help people sustain freedom to live the sorts of lives they want? If their bodies restrict them from certain activities, how might we bring ease or comfort into their lives or help them achieve an alternate means for staying active and engaged? If certain tasks are demanding for them, are there innovative solutions that could ease their burden? And if they want help, how might we create an environment where it's easy to ask for such help while preserving their dignity?

For my parents, in moving into a congregate living residence, they took a great deal of comfort from simply not having to cook and then they found real pleasure in sharing meals with newfound friends. For the individual who has had a lifelong devotion to physical exercise, sustaining that ritual in a body that is weaker than it used to be might mean providing them a swimming pool and an instructor to guide their exercise or substituting a state-of-the-art stationary bike and an interactive virtual system once they can no longer safely ride outdoors. Let's make their new homes as attractive, welcoming, and sunlit as possible. Provide the amenities that cater to the activities they desire to pursue; facilitate their ability to continue to participate in social clubs and volunteer activities in the larger community; give them ready access to safe, beautiful outdoor environments; give them a seat at the table so that they can participate in the governance of their residential communities and so that they have a say in what happens within them. If the old are caretakers of our culture and our collective history, let's become the caretakers of their freedom.

To do so, we must also take care of those who take care of them. Those who work with seniors are extraordinarily passionate about what they do. Most see enriching seniors' lives as their calling. Many seek to continue their formal education in order to provide the best care possible. Many are quick to volunteer for extra shifts or to participate in extracurricular activities that benefit their residents. During COVID-19, the vast majority of senior sector workers were willing to place their own lives and their own health on the line to make certain that their residents were safe and that they never felt abandoned. Because they give so much, we have to make certain that we treat our workforce with the dignity and respect they deserve. We need to maximize their benefits whenever possible and pay them on a scale commiserate with their experience, qualifications, and responsibilities. We need to provide them the tools, technologies, and safety equipment they need to perform their jobs at their best. We need to provide them work environments that are comfortable, inviting, and inspiring, and we need to give them places within residences where they can decompress and attend to personal needs that are comfortable and well appointed. In short, we need to treat our employees with the same humanism with which we treat our residents.

I speak of residents and team members and caregivers. You might speak of customers and employees. It's still the same conversation.

Many of the needs of our caregivers and those for whom they provide run parallel to one another. The better we design and appoint the residences we operate, the more all will recognize that these buildings are people's homes. They need to be designed with features that are both inviting and functional. For example, we must make certain that the homes we provide our residents are specifically constructed not only to meet the requirements of wheelchairs, electric scooters, and walkers but also account for the movement, storage, and operational needs of such devices. When planning and developing new properties, we improve the outcomes for all when we design in ways that maximize the independence of our residents. When they do need additional help, we should design in a manner conducive to ease and respectful assistance from our team members.

We must recognize that at the same time older people deserve independence, dignity, and self-governance, they are members of a demographic that is more vulnerable than others. Because such vulnerability—due to greater susceptibility to viruses and bacteria, greater likelihood to sustain injury from falls, more targeting by criminals and those perpetrating financial scams, higher dependence on others because of limited mobility—is an undeniable reality, we must reach a balance between providing seniors with safety and access to healthcare while also preserving their rights and honouring their decisions. And if individuals no longer have the cognitive ability to make decisions that ensure their own health and safety, we must gather input from their family and medical experts and consult directives they have placed in writing prior to cognitive decline.

We honour the older people of our society by creating environments that address what Pearl Buck wrote about in *The Good Earth* when she said, "Our society must make it right and possible for old people not to fear the young or be deserted by them." Indeed, we should develop opportunities where younger people interact with older people regularly and have the chance to become friends. Equality can happen only when it's personal, when we form individual relationships that make us step beyond herd thinking. The simple act of spending time with someone from a different generation is a powerful way to keep prejudice from forming, especially when you're young, which is exactly when most of our prejudices are formed. This can be as direct as has been tried in The Netherlands and Sweden, where college students live rent-free in senior housing residences. Or it can be educational at the same time it forges intergenerational relationships, as is the case in a partnership initiative formed between Revera and Reel Youth, a Vancouver nonprofit that helps young Canadians tell stories through film. With the Age Is More Film Project, we have paired students with seniors in our retirement communities and have produced more than 280 short films that celebrate older Canadians and bring together what used to be the two solitudes of young and old.

A collaborative program like the Age is More Film Project features innovation in action. It is derived from a problem-solving focus and simultaneously helps two groups in need. It matches youth who show tremendous promise but who often lack opportunity with seniors who have a zest for wanting to meet new people and talk about new ideas but who can, by the very way we've structured our society, feel isolated and dismissed as irrelevant. It uses a medium that creates powerful emotional impact, one that registers for young people as familiar and intriguing while also providing them technological skill development, critical thinking strategies, communication skills, and practiced engagement with strangers that can serve them all the rest of their lives. The product that emerges can be shared with families and friends and enjoyed again and again. The films generate pleasure at the same time they prove instructional. A program such as this one with Reel Youth showcases many of the expectations of innovation and the entrepreneurial spirit that cements a vision dedicated to positive change.

The Age Is More program highlights an approach that guides much of the action we have taken at Revera. In 2015, Revera launched the five-year Innovators in Aging initiative that I've drawn on elsewhere to offer illustrations of innovation in action. Here was the promise we made our residents, our employees, and our board when it launched:

- We would select up to twenty innovators who fit the specific criteria of helping residents, families, and team members in our communities.

- Those innovators would come into our communities to pilot their latest products and services, on a much larger scale—and in a real-world environment—than they had access to before. We would create systems to provide feedback from focus groups who would represent those who could benefit from the innovation.

- We would commit $20 million to invest in the innovators who emerged.

In addition to working with innovators in whom we might invest, Revera empowers our employees to find solutions that elevate the resident experience and enhance care and services.

The premise was quite straightforward. Beyond seeing opportunity to improve lives through new services and new technologies, we found that more and more seniors were taking an active approach to defining what they needed to improve their lives and were more active in sharing how they wanted to live their lives. The project represents a tremendous opportunity for Canadian businesses that choose to focus on innovations for the senior market. With Canadians living well into their eighties and nineties, Revera recommended that companies rethink how they view the senior market and understand that a person who is eighty-five years old has different wants and needs from someone in their early seventies. Turning to innovators to help develop solutions for older adults' concerns about health or lost independence offered a classic alignment between opportunity and need. Indeed, the outputs of this program, much like the design behind it, offer a worthy kind of case study in applied innovation.

It started with putting our money where our mouth was. In addition to inviting entrepreneurs to pitch their ideas for products and services, we took other steps to make certain that our residents had the means to share their experiences and perspectives. This was an extension of the thinking that had led us to create the chief elder officer position. Hiring Hazel ensured that residents had an engaged, energetic, experienced advocate with a role in senior management, access to our board and to provincial and national government officials, and a powerful voice to engage with the public when discussing the issues most relevant to them. The decision to create a chief elder officer arose from the same thinking that led us to form a chief medical officer position, the first in the senior living sector in Canada, in order to make certain that all policies, programs, and communications that had direct relevance to the medical concerns of our residents had an authority's final point of responsibility at the most senior level of our organization. The thinking behind seeing benefits in such a position is why we formed a senior position for a chief innovation officer. Without the leadership and centralized focus on innovation, it's hard to create the level of commitment and impact that can expand an innovative mindset throughout a large enterprise.

Investment in these positions was fundamental to a larger, innovative program we have termed "More Living," which operates on the basic principle that if we can help residents simplify their lives or reduce the things that cause them stress or dissipate their energy, we can help them focus on other pursuits that bring more meaning and greater pleasure.

What were some of these innovations? Let me introduce a few to illustrate the kinds of thinking that went on behind these business decisions. Our decisions can prove instructive to how you might imagine changes you can implement to impact your own customers and help you seize competitive advantage.

With Innovators in Aging, we did things like test a wearable sensor that helps identify seniors at risk of falls, recognizing that fall prevention is one of the most impactful ways we can improve seniors' lives. Falls are the leading cause of both fatal and nonfatal injuries for people over age sixty-five. Falls can result in hip fractures, broken bones, and head injuries. They often become event markers that lead to other medical complications like injury-site infections or worsen other conditions. Even falls without a major injury can cause an older adult to become fearful or depressed. Trying to prevent falls became important to design features we implemented when we developed new properties, resulting in practices like employing integrated motion sensor track lighting to provide clear pathways to bathrooms in senior apartments, removing trip hazards, and offering walk-in shower stalls, among many other features.

Sometimes those unique wants and needs include finding the means to improve memory or reduce a sense of loneliness, which is why we invested in Rendever, which uses virtual reality experiences designed to spark new conversations and reduce social isolation. Residents can use the Rendever virtual reality software alone or as a shared experience with other residents or families. The software is customizable and can assist reminiscence therapy by allowing a resident to revisit their childhood home, wedding location, or anywhere from their past. They can now check items off their remaining bucket list without ever leaving the safety of their home.

Often the technology we've tested is, like Rendever, pretty mind-blowing in the seemingly futuristic ways it can enhance the living experience. If you don't work in the senior sector, you'd likely be astounded by the kinds of innovative, helpful technologies, products, and services available, from personal health companions that include pill dispensers to blind spot sensors for wheelchairs, from devices that alert family members to significant changes in their loved one's sleep patterns to an assistive device designed to relieve hand tremors that may result from essential tremor or Parkinson's disease. I'm sure I would be equally amazed at innovations in sectors with which I have no experience.

Sometimes innovation in back-office functions can have even larger benefits for our residents than these more consumer-direct technologies. I've already discussed elsewhere the many benefits we have realized from our investment in BookJane. Its impacts are similar to those we have realized by partnering with Cubigo. Cubigo connects team members, residents, and family members by digitizing common resident community functions like dining, maintenance, transportation, communication, and activities. Not only does this simple-to-use platform make it easy for residents to request or schedule activities and appointments, it incorporates digital signage throughout our properties. That can benefit our team members as much as our residents, and for those of us on the corporate side, we have seen improved workflows and lowered operating costs while also gathering loads of useful data than can provide us valuable insights. Its abilities can extend to families, offering them useful ways not only to check on their loved one's appointments but also to connect to their caregivers.

Another investment has been pivotal in shaping how we hire team members. Using big data and predictive analytics, Arena identifies the candidates who will best impact our organization and are most likely to thrive in a specific role, department, and location. By applying the power of analytics, we have been able to remove unconscious bias from the hiring process and have increased retention, which has a huge impact not only on reducing the costs of training but also in helping to shape the kind of culture we have worked hard to develop.

All of the innovations I have briefly highlighted are fascinating on their own, and each of the entrepreneurs behind them have fantastic stories. Most have been through many trials and tribulations to realize their vision and bring their products to the market. I'd be negligent if I suggested that there are not significant challenges faced in getting innovations from the pilot phase to broad operational adaptation across a large and diverse network such as Revera. There are very real barriers you must cross in order to implement even the best ideas and products. Some of those challenges come from working with entrepreneurs who may not yet have made the evolution from start-up to full-scale business. Other can arrive because of the scale of our corporation and the differing needs from operation to operation. At times, even among the best entrepreneurs, the explosive growth that can come from partnering with a corporation of our scale can overwhelm manufacturing capacity. And sometimes, despite careful due diligence, potential investment partners might not be up to the task or may not embrace innovation with the same enthusiasm we have.

The reason I have taken the time to share several of the innovations we have attempted is to provide a picture of what is possible when you begin to ask what solutions you *could* apply rather than dwell on what feels impossible. Curious-minded people are always capable of imagining solutions that, at their inception, can seem impossible. Hopefully, examples we have implemented at Revera can send your mind reeling with imagining how the needs of your own industry might be met with creative thinking, collaboration with others who possess imaginative problem-solving natures, and a will to try to contribute to a world in which you are always striving to move ahead.

The kind of thinking that our innovation partners demonstrate goes hand in glove with *why* we formed the Innovators in Aging initiative in the first place. They truly represent the kinds of imaginative thinking that can solve problems like ageism. We live in a time of tremendous social change, one where people all around the world reject prejudicial behaviours. It is beyond time that the call of equity and social justice extends to seniors. We can have no tolerance for ageism. We can no longer see older people as irrelevant or dismiss them as having passed the time of their lives when they were vital to the larger cultural exchange. Kindness, like intelligence, is not age discriminant. Living with purpose does not stop at an arbitrary marker of a birth date. Often the process of change can feel slow, and too often it inflicts confusion and pain as those slow to accept it hold on to false narratives of the past. We can be at the forefront of positive change or look back and lament our ignorance.

If we can make this change in our collective vision now, when we are all eighty or ninety or one hundred, we will benefit from the same independence and freedom of choice we take for granted today. Applying innovation will shorten the path to achieving that end.

CHAPTER 8

# ARE YOU APPLYING INNOVATION?

- Have you made innovation a priority by budgeting specifically for it or by creating initiatives that incentivize innovative approaches?

- What are the biggest problems in your industry that need solving? Have you identified entrepreneurs who are focused on solving aspects of those problems?

- Have you placed someone in charge of seeking out innovation within and outside of your company? What are the ways that you monitor the development of new technologies that can impact your industry?

- Do the innovations that you focus on in your company have direct impact on your customers?

- Do you have mechanisms in place to seek out feedback from those who would be most affected by the implementation of a new technology or new service?

- Is your culture supportive of failure versus perfection on the path to excellence?

- Do you have the ability to see your business from your customer's point of view? Do you make it a practice to do so with each decision that you make?

# PART 3

# Humans Serving Humans: Realizing Excellence by Developing Cultures of Respect, Integrity, and Compassion

# Craft a Culture: Creating the Workplace That Would Make Our Parents Proud

Whenever I visit one of our retirement residences or long-term care homes, one of the first things I ask my host is to see the team members' staff room. In my early years at Revera, as had been the case at CML, these rooms were nearly always in the basement. Most were dark and dingy. Frequently they were cluttered and poorly maintained. They were not at all the sorts of places where you would want to take your breaks or prepare to start your shift. These rooms are, of course, used daily by our frontline teams, whose hands are the ones that, literally, touch our residents. In healthcare we are a people serving people business. Without frontline teams, we would not have a business at all. They are our personal support workers, our cleaners, our nurses and therapists, our cooks and custodians. It was little wonder to me that most of the team members I met when visiting residences weren't terribly enthusiastic about our company culture. I couldn't blame them. Having a clean, inviting staff room offers a clear message of respect. In those first years leading the company, I set about, with the support of our operational leadership team, to making sure that we changed their atmosphere, moving them to aboveground floors where possible, providing more lighting, and creating more inviting spaces. We've renovated many, and whenever we build new properties, we pay special attention to how we design these rooms by creating atmospheres that are respectful, comforting, and welcoming.

Paying attention to the spaces where our team members gather may seem minor, but it demonstrates a great deal about our values, and it has an unconscious effect on team member morale and their vision of the company and their jobs. It also demonstrates the concept of leadership that is encapsulated in the phrase, "You heard, you said, and you did," which enables you to walk the talk on accountability across a culture. More important than the physical outlay of the room or site is the fact that we have taken the time to respect the space as a place of solitude and recovery, which in turn links back to our business culture.

These ideas extend to our residents as well, just as they should for your customers. I sincerely doubt that any of us would want our parent or spouse to live in a belowground room without natural light or one that is dated or dirty. Is there any clearer signal of disrespect or perceived inequality than a poorly equipped or neglected workspace? Mutual and genuine respect is a cornerstone of the kind of culture I want to create in the organizations I lead.

Think of your own business interactions just within your immediate neighbourhood. You likely have the luxury of choice for where you spend your money. What businesses do you frequent and why? I'd wager that your choices start with quality and efficiency and then move beyond those to variants like the friendliness of the team members, the pleasant nature of the environment, the sense that you feel valued and welcomed as a customer. When an owner takes pride in the business—pays attention to its aesthetics, keeps a restroom spotless, uses products from other local businesses—don't you feel a kind of pride as a regular customer? Doesn't it become "your" coffee-house or "your" health club? Don't we want our employees to feel that pride as well and have it impact how they conduct themselves at work?

We can't go about designing and developing the behaviours we want to see in teams until we know what kind of culture we hope to establish. It means thinking about how we want the company to be perceived by the public. It means knowing what kind of climate we want to work in. And it means reaching out to see what sort of climate our teams desire. Our vision of a desired workplace environment cannot be realized if we don't first consider the kind of place our customers want to do business, or in the case of Revera, the kind of place where people want to live. Culture eats strategy for lunch, so if you can't get the cultural connection, you can forget about your great strategy.

This all starts with the "say hello" principle introduced early on. We cannot underestimate the power of simple daily actions: greet people, show respect, be kind, demonstrate interest in our coworkers, lend a hand, ask questions. These actions are contagious. Just as toxicity can spread through a company, so can civility. See your job as a spreader of civility and it will pay back exponentially. Hear Aretha Franklin's voice: "R-E-S-P-E-C-T." I want to spend my days where people work hard but laugh with regularity. Entering such a workplace makes me want to contribute the best of what I can offer, and that in turn positions me to be far more receptive of divergent ideas and differing perspectives.

# Follow Your Compass

I have spent considerable time and energy thinking about the experiences of my life—at work, at home, growing up, and among the influence of those I've learned from. I think about those people and experiences as I make decisions. I think about such reflection as following my compass. The moral, humanistic influences that guide the person I want to be also guide the CEO I want to become.

> **Any organization is bettered when it takes advantage of the collective wisdom of its members.**

At the core of those beliefs is this: Any organization is bettered when it takes advantage of the collective wisdom of its members. For me, central to creating an effective culture is to try to achieve one that is as nonhierarchical as possible, one that fosters a spirit of openness where people feel safe and comfortable and have confidence that they can ask questions and share ideas. I want a workplace where it is acceptable, even desirable, to ask your boss legitimate, tough questions.

The delicate balancing act is making sure that employees knowingly believe they are heard and supported while also creating an environment where everyone understands that decisions have to be made and then all must align behind such decisions. No good comes to a workplace where decisions are second-guessed. If people believe they've been heard and their input is taken seriously, a lot of the second-guessing disappears. Decisions should be viewed as decisions, not as personal affronts. There's no win/loss column on whether your idea gets implemented, but we must make certain that every idea is considered. It takes effort and purpose to create such a culture, once again going back to the "you heard, you said, and you did" orientation to demonstrate the commitment.

Because I have spent considerable time working in numerous different cultures—in Canada, the United Kingdom, Germany, most of the EU accession countries, Asia, and the United States—where broader cultural values impact the nature of how businesses operate and how people interact together, that's helped me understand the kinds of workplace cultures that can exist within a business as well. Similar to how ethnic or national cultures can evolve over time and reflect the values and behaviours of those people bound to them, businesses can begin to reflect the people who work within them and their attitudes about their work, about other people with whom they work, and about the people they serve.

# Motivation

When you speak about culture, whether within an individual business or within a broad collection of people with shared roots, it's hard to avoid some stereotyping, but typically some of the values do apply to a majority. Individuals will always defy generalizations, but patterns emerge. For example, speaking as someone who came up in business through the sales and marketing ranks at Eli Lilly, I can attest that in an atmosphere driven by meeting quotas and sales goals and compensation that is often incentivized by commissions, there exists a naturally competitive spirit that in the wrong hands can become cutthroat. It is important to monitor competitiveness and to create a balance between the individual and the team.

Whatever your business may be, it's likely that it has either taken on the personality of some of its leaders or that it applies cultural imperatives derived from the nature of the work completed there. As I have discussed earlier, in the senior care and retirement industry, because our teams care so genuinely about the well-being of our residents, they are quick to volunteer to work additional hours and take on more responsibilities. Our industry requires a deep empathetic fibre. Our teams are not unlike schoolteachers who buy supplies with their own money in order to make sure all their students have similar opportunities. Their primary motivations are outwardly focused, and the rewards are often intrinsic. That is why respect and recognition for their skills of empathetically caring for the aging population are so important.

This vision of cultural personalities, if you will, is often easier to see when working among broader, more traditional cultural populations. For example, during my years working as the president of Lilly Germany, it became almost immediately clear how much our German employees valued their families. While families in Germany tend to be small, they place a lot of value on the importance of their children. This is reflected in many German governmental policies, such as lengthy paid family leave.

While rooted in another generalization, in my experience working in a German business environment, there were many smart, inventive Germans loaded with great ideas, but they were scared to step forward due to the culture of fear in the organization, almost as if the culture was one of being told what to do or that there was no trust. When I started leading the German operation of Eli Lilly, it had not delivered on its business plan for several years. As a Canadian, the challenge was therefore to push my team to think strategically, but in Germany we needed to establish a culture of trust by being accountable to financial benchmarks and fulfilling our commitments to the broader corporation. In order to try to motivate our German team to shift their thinking and embrace accountability, we created a challenge. We discussed this with our senior leadership team, and I promised the team that if they would help develop a business plan and then hit the numbers put forth in it for the year, we'd celebrate with a family-oriented Christmas event.

Now if there's another stereotype that holds up under scrutiny about the Germans, it's that they *love* Christmas. Germany is, after all, the birthplace of St. Nicholas and of the tradition of Christmas trees. The custom of the Weihnachtsmarkt, or Christmas markets, fairy-tale-like seasonal markets filled with rides and games, lights and market stalls, is cherished. My promise was that if we executed our business plan and delivered on our commitment to the broader corporate good, we would create our own company Weihnachtsmarkt. All of our teams across the organization rose to the challenge, and we invited all of them and their families to the top of a mountain where we celebrated the season and their success. That promise had become a significant motivator. For many Germans, the kind of work and commitment that went into creating a family-oriented Christmas market dedicated to them was more meaningful than a year-end financial bonus. I still remember the blustery December night that we celebrated together in a tent strapped to the top of the Feldberg Mountains and toasted each other with Glühwein.

I share such a story because it demonstrates something critical about culture—different people are motivated by different incentives. A salesman is probably going to thrive on a head-to-head sales competition, but a social worker might be as motivated if the result of their success is the funding of a program that will benefit their clients.

# THE CEO AS MASTER GARDENER

I liken my job as a CEO to gardening. With planning, a lot of work, and some love, you can create a beautiful, productive garden, one that's nice to spend time in and full of healthy plants that offer a bountiful harvest. But one lesson the gardener learns early is that you can't control all the elements—weather and insects and animals— so you have to adapt. Even the best-laid plans can be upended by a late frost or an early snow. And over time you learn other lessons, like if you're not diligent, watering and fertilizing with regularity, and if you're not weeding your beds or rotating where you plant different species over the years and renewing the soil, your garden shows the neglect, your productivity declines, and plants go to seed or become ungainly. If not tended to and reinvigorated with regularity, you won't be able to harvest so many healthy vegetables or beautiful flowers, and it's simply no longer such a pleasant place to work.

Like gardens, businesses require that you constantly observe, recheck, and renew them to keep them healthy. Any of the extensions of this metaphor apply to your business, whether you need to weed out those people who can't adapt to new demands or you must make certain you pour on the motivational energy and recognition that remind people how much they matter. It means figuring out ways to check in with the garden and observe its progress, to look under the leaves for aphids, if you will. As your business grows, it will be harder to reach out to remote sites or to sit down with frontline workers, but you have to find the time and you have to train those managers and senior leaders you task with oversight to do the same and report their findings. And just as there are times when you have to put down the tools and simply take in the garden in its bounty, you've got to stop and listen to the hum of your business—the conversations among employees outside of meetings, the tone and accuracy of reports and memos, the interactions with your customers. You have to review the annual cycle of the garden, see which crops were successful and which ones failed, try to establish why, and record those learnings for future reference. And you've got to celebrate, as a community of "gardeners," the rituals of those annual cycles and recognize that just as everyone working together gets to reap the rewards of the harvest, they've all got to pull together and plant the seeds that will start each cycle.

You won't know what mechanisms to use in order to motivate your teams if you don't understand the corporate culture that currently exists and the one you want to encourage. Sometimes this takes creativity. On the heels of success from our Weihnachtsmarkt, we raised our stakes exponentially and committed to something long wanted and never achieved for the German team: a new office building—"ein neues Bürogebäude." My commitment to the team was that if we met our business plan metrics for two years in a row, we'd build a new German headquarters. I succeeded in getting corporate backing for the building, and we set about developing the strategic plan to accomplish our yearly strategic goal. Germans show a strong appreciation of architecture and value working in energizing, efficient, and beautiful work environments. It was easy to get buy-in with this motivational tool.

At one point we gathered four hundred employees in a tent on the new building site, and with the help of an industrial installation artist from Hamburg, we erected a metal artistic tree that measured twenty-five feet tall. The leaves of the tree were made from copper, and all four hundred people present were able to shape and cut copper leaves to affix to the sculpture. They imprinted the leaves with words and metaphors that, individualized by each of them, captured the regrowth they envisioned for our collective future business strategy and their images of what could be achieved within this new building. The tree gave people an emotional and tactile way to feel like they had participated in building something bigger than themselves. The completed tree now stands outside the finished building at Werner-Reimers-Starsse in Bad Homburg, Germany.

## Learning to Listen

Through this motivational experience, we'd helped foster a sense of ownership in the company's future and an implicit commitment to listening to the collective. Of course, to listen to the collective, you've got to create a culture where people actively listen. It takes conscientious purpose to hear colleagues, not only to hear the ideas they communicate but also to recognize and understand the perspective they bring, whether that perspective has been formed through the division of the company they represent, the expertise they bring to the project, their past relevant experience, or personal attributes. As leaders, we not only have to train ourselves to be active listeners who pick up on visual and nonvisual cues when interacting with team members but also make sure that we manage meetings in ways that individuals don't dominate discussion and that the quieter voices in the room have the opportunity to be heard. We have to recognize that many people are intimidated by hierarchy and title and hesitant to share their ideas with senior managers. While it's important that we don't create chaos by letting people leapfrog communications beyond their teams and supervisors, we need to develop a balanced atmosphere where we're available to our teams and where we have systems in place to ensure that good ideas always have channels by which they can reach the most senior team members.

To reach equilibrium on such a balance beam, you don't just have to be open to new ideas; you have to create a culture that supports uncomfortable thinking. That means making sure new ideas don't get shot down—again this requires trust and confidence. Individuals need to be allowed agency. People need to know that their colleagues will listen to them. They need to have confidence that discussions will be open, that they will be rigorous, that ideas will be challenged, and that conclusions won't be reached without the support of evidence and data. We need environments where fledgling ideas that prove to have value are given the space to evolve through brainstorming, collaboration, and equality in the division of needed actions that emerge. That requires us to be confident enough to admit we do not have all the answers.

# Creating Culture

So how do we build a culture that acts on such ideals? We start by making certain we emulate the traits we want to see throughout the company. If we don't practice what we preach, the values we want to foster will never trickle down. Second, we have to be absolutely clear in communicating our expectations.

**If we don't practice what we preach, the values we want to foster will never trickle down.**

Culture is not created overnight. It has to be cultivated and reinforced. Another approach to such reinforcement is regular use of auditing focused on finding learnings that emerge from past performances. By capturing what you have learned, you can reemphasize how collaborative, open sharing has created success, how that was accomplished, and how it was fostered. It is imperative to focus on both the what and the why.

A final element to creating an open culture is building in accountability. It's an old cliché but an accurate one that to whom much is given, much is expected. I want people on our teams to feel empowered as fully engaged participants in guiding the direction of the company and implementing our strategic initiatives. I want them to enjoy coming to work and feel that they are contributing to something bigger than themselves. But this means that they must be accountable for their actions and communications. If we are really going to listen and speak openly, it also means that we have to speak clearly when we make mistakes or don't deliver on commitments. We have to eliminate blame culture. Rather than attribute blame, we must support colleagues when they step up and assume responsibility for the work they have done. We're never going to be perfect, but we need to own our actions and speak honestly with one another about where we need to improve. In short, we must look at constant learning through objectivity on truly understanding the "why" behind a win or a loss.

When all the measures I've outlined don't work, there's a good reason, one that you probably identified early on but wanted to believe you could transform—the recalcitrant or wrongly placed leader. It's a simple but harsh truth of cultivating culture, one that every culture—business or otherwise—has confronted throughout the history of our species: Some individuals refuse to follow the norms established by the majority. When those individuals are in positions of authority, they can roadblock all the hard work you've put in. I certainly believe in giving people a chance to evolve into new expectations, but if they fail to be a productive fit in moving the collective forward, a leader has to be willing to remove them. To retain people in leadership positions who don't agree with your company's strategic destination or with the compass headings that will allow you to arrive there puts the entire expedition at risk.

Although we spend time and effort to attract leaders to and retain them in our business, people can become disengaged or start to model poor behaviours. It's important that we are constantly re-evaluating and providing support and feedback to our direct team reports. There have been a number of times during my career when I've had to make difficult decisions and leadership changes in the hopes of bettering the business. During COVID-19, the needs of the business even meant releasing and hiring high-level leaders in remote locations because closed borders meant I could not take these actions in person; the business interests were so compelling that I had to take action even if circumstances were less than ideal. To be able to take such action demanded that I had regular contact with senior leaders across the organization, loads of performance data, and an informed overview of our international operations.

Making these kinds of personnel changes is never easy. In some cases, it may be due to consistent lack of performance; in other cases, it may be due to the nature of the strategy of the business; and finally, and most importantly, it might have to do with a cultural or values misfit between the individual and the company. There have been a number of situations when I wish I had moved sooner to make a leadership change. So often difficult changes are necessary to move the team forward. It's important when you feel that itch in your stomach or the twinge on the back of your neck that you go with your gut and make the difficult decisions as respectfully but as expeditiously as possible. It is better for the collective if you do.

Creating a workplace culture that retains the strongest assets among our people and generates the best, most innovative ideas and strategies takes time, consistent work, and consistent focus. But there's a major payoff when we do, for in cultures where people feel valued and are excited to participate, there's a through line to innovation. If you study the history of humans, you see with consistency that the cultures that are the most entrepreneurial and that generate the highest quality of life are the ones in which their citizens are the most participatory. My own country of Canada is a great example of a purposeful attempt to provide the means for participation and financial gain by empowering more people. It's a proud and central spirit on which our nation was founded. We all possess the capacity for creative thinking. You've certainly experienced the energy in a room where a lot of people with creative thoughts join together to focus on problem-solving. As diverse viewpoints are shared, the strongest, most applicable ideas percolate to the centre of discussion and, with the guidance of skilled leaders, move toward actionable agendas. That's the spirit at the root of the workplace culture I'm talking about.

I've seen this kind of culture evolve. And I'll be the first to admit that it is an evolutionary process, one that is always a work in progress. At Revera, we've had a lot of success in transforming workplace culture by concentrating our efforts on our core vision and our core values, encouraging everyone to go above and beyond every day. It's the sort of commitment for which we have been recognized and rewarded, including being named one of "Canada's Most Admired Corporate Cultures" in 2019 by Waterstone Human Capital.

In this chapter I've shared with you some of the values I place a premium on in cultivating the kind of workplace culture that can provide both satisfaction and a competitive advantage. The next job is up to you, and that is to determine the kind of culture you value and want to foster in the organization you lead.

# WHAT KIND OF CULTURE DO YOU WANT?

Because cultures typically take on the attributes of their leaders, as any quick survey of world history will remind you, the culture you desire is usually the one you'll get. But how much thought have you given to the sort of work environment you want to shape?

- What are three cultural attributes you want your business to actively reflect?

- What personal behaviours are part of your own day-to-day interactions that you'd like to see others in your organization emulate? What ones would you be wise to keep consciously in check?

- How would you describe the current workplace culture in your enterprise?

- What mechanisms have you put in place to make sure your people have the chance to have their ideas shared?

- Who in your organization is responsible for overseeing that communications are shared with consistency of message and tone?

- Are you walking the talk—"We heard, we said, and we did"?

CHAPTER 10

# Strive for Excellence: Achieving Perfection Is Impossible but Worth Attempting

As highlighted at the end of the last chapter, a central part of the culture we are trying to develop is a commitment to striving to achieve excellence across the entirety of our enterprise. It's been my experience, however, that too often people mistake attempting to achieve excellence with an expectation of perfection. As the subtitle for this chapter suggests, attempting perfection is a worthy goal. But realistically, it

163

needs to stay a goal, or, to use the language I've applied elsewhere, a useful bearing for your compass. Perfection is impossible. Don't lower your standards, but accept that in the search for excellence, you're going to make mistakes. Let me quote a fellow Canadian, someone who, over the course of his long, productive life, fashioned powerful messages as a musician and writer, Leonard Cohen: "Ring the bell that still can ring / Forget the perfect offering / There is a crack, a crack in everything / That's how the light gets in." Cohen understood

**Too often people mistake attempting to achieve excellence with an expectation of perfection.**

that everything in the world is flawed but was wise enough to know that it is in such flaws that we see beauty and wonder and humanity. As he says in his song "Anthem," such flaws are "where the light gets in." If we want to translate that phrase in a corporate setting, we can see the places where the light gets in as problems that need solving, systems that need improving, and opportunities to do good. I focused an earlier chapter on doing what you do well. The inverse is also important: know your weaknesses (at the personal and the organizational levels) and put effort into improving them.

Permit me to quote another Canadian, the actor Michael J. Fox, who said, "I am careful not to confuse excellence with perfection. Excellence, I can reach for; perfection is God's business." That's a good mantra. We should always strive for excellence. Indeed, we must hold ourselves, our businesses, and our people to the highest standards of excellence. But we can't afford to let a desire to attain excellence get in the way of forward momentum. Nor can we confuse excellence with perfection.

For me, it comes down to a simple mindset. As I talk with collaborators, whether those are our team or leaders of another enterprise with which we have formed a partnership, I emphasize that I don't want to hear the fifty reasons why something won't work. I want to hear the one reason why it might. The ability to consider a potential solution rather than dwell on the problem is precisely why I place such value in those with inquisitive minds. The creative thinker is inspired by problems because they see problems simply as things requiring solutions. They like challenges. They find energy in applying ingenious approaches to concerns others expend energy worrying about. I see such thinking at the core of innovation and a reason we have to promote and celebrate creative thinking among our employees and look for it in the people we hire.

Without such thinking, you cannot grow in meaningful ways. As I have emphasized throughout this book, the world is constantly changing, so the solutions required must change as well. If that weren't the case, then we could simply put our businesses on cruise control and rely on dividends by doing the same thing we've been doing for the last fifty years. When you find the business that's been successful at doing that, let me know.

Yet it's hard to admit that we haven't perfected our business. I've spoken elsewhere about the need for leaders to show their vulnerabilities and accept that they don't have all the answers. They must be willing to show that they want to learn new things. They have to show evidence that they are not fearful of making mistakes. The companies they lead have to demonstrate the same qualities. At some point, your business will literally run out of growth potential if it does only one thing, even if it does that thing better than anyone else. When Apple still focused entirely on the PC business, it nearly went bankrupt despite producing what many regarded as the superior personal computer. It resurrected the business by shifting most of its focus to refine its various devices in a closed ecosystem of cloud services. To be successful at such a transformation, a company has to do what's uncomfortable and to learn what it doesn't yet know.

You can't learn new things if you get caught up in a belief in perfection. A closer look at that famous Apple example will remind us that Steve Jobs spent a lot of his early career obsessed with perfection. His obsession with detail delayed getting the original Apple McIntosh to market by three years. In those three years, the market had largely changed, and Microsoft's hold on operating systems had infiltrated nearly every business sector and they had built deals with nearly every PC manufacturer. Jobs never stopped wanting to finesse every detail of Apple products, but he let go much of his control and stayed focused on excellence rather than on attempting perfection.

Let me provide an example of the value that comes with getting uncomfortable from my own experience. Revera had a long history and a great deal of expertise as a real estate company, owning and managing operating properties. A primary focus of my time as its CEO has been to take the steps to ensure that we have evolved to provide for the needs of the residents who live in those communities better than anyone else in the senior living sector. Have we reached perfection? Certainly not, but we do aim for it and we do achieve excellence. But one of the things we had not done before with any real focus was to bring our real estate excellence and our senior living excellence together to become a property developer. We owned a lot of land assets and knew the ins and outs of completing real estate transactions. We had learned over experience what our residents wanted and needed, and we knew the operational components of the physical properties where they lived. Despite all this knowledge, it remained a daunting prospect to tackle the challenge of developing and building a property from scratch.

We entered our first Revera-only development venture with a lens on what we thought would enhance the resident experience. We wanted to take our existing understanding of residents' needs and imagine a future of possibilities. That started a process of translating our findings into our development concept for the premium/luxury market segment. We'd been strategic in gathering and applying data about our physical facilities, so we had a good start on a development mentality. Moreover, we had benefited from the experience we gained from our investment into Sunrise Senior Living in the US and then subsequently having acquired a UK company called Signature Senior Lifestyles. Both of these businesses had in-house teams with development experience serving a high-end assisted living clientele/market segment.

We quickly learned that the kinds of construction experience we had from past remodeling, renovation, and infrastructure upgrades was still a far cry from what you had to know as a developer contending with land and zoning regulations at the provincial and local level or how to best manage construction partners. We made a lot of mistakes along the way. But we learned from those mistakes. If we'd waited around until we had every aspect of the design or every bit of the process perfect, we would probably still be the proud owners of four prime, empty acres in the Toronto suburbs. Instead, teams pulled together, operations supported construction, construction supported operations, and now that 137-unit property, Westney Gardens, is full, and residents share their satisfaction with the choice to call it home. We weren't perfect, but we pushed ourselves toward excellence, and we moved forward diligently. We didn't stall. Developing that property gave us a growing knowledge base that has now allowed us to expand. That successful track record has attracted more investment funds and institutional capital to Revera. By differentiating excellence from perfection, we were able to achieve something special.

That ability to differentiate the two is something that you have to inculcate in your culture. It has to become a mindset across your entire organization, not just in pockets. There are a couple of key steps you have to take to get there.

> **By differentiating excellence from perfection, we were able to achieve something special.**

First, you have to transform people's definition of failure. I'm not suggesting that we want to aspire to failure, but if you are taking risks, even calculated ones, occasional failure is inevitable. There are a lot of trite clichés that suggest you have to fail in order succeed. I don't know about that. But I do like what André Agassi said: "When your company is growing, what is most pleasing? The first billion or ten billion? No. I assure you the best part of being with a great company is being able to work, push yourself individually daily, and engage in the participation. Failure and success are an illusion. Failure is not an event; it is the interpretation of an event." What do we do with mistakes? As leaders, do we model the behaviours of how we communicate bad news? Has our company created an apparatus to support learning when inevitable mistakes happen? To echo the Leonard Cohen lyrics I used to introduce this chapter, I think about the James Joyce quotation: "Mistakes are the portals of discovery."

# Eradicating Blame Culture While Maintaining Accountability

Your company will never be successful if it employs a blame culture. In too many companies, when something goes wrong, leaders look for someone to pin the failure on and then make an example of punishing them. If we're intent on making personnel changes when things fall apart, we're far better off to remove those who go around looking to cast blame. They are not moving the company forward. They become a cancer that eats away at morale and productivity. Such people's singular interest is in protecting themselves, and we need to have no tolerance for them in our businesses. I'm far more interested in investing in those who own up to an error when they make it and who then get busy fixing the problem. Good leaders invite scrutiny, reflection, and discussion on how to avoid repeating mistakes. Success has many mothers and fathers, but failure is an orphan.

The reflection I speak of must be intentional. It goes far beyond encouraging employees to examine the outcomes of projects and initiatives. You have to make reflective debriefing activities a structured part of your process, one so expected within your culture that it becomes second nature. For such exercises to be successful, all the other elements of culture I've spoken about also have to be in place, for to deconstruct the factors that created any outcome—successful or not—your team has to be able to communicate with honesty in an environment where there will be no blameful repercussions and no judgment cast. You are not looking in the mirror to admire yourself; you're planning an adjustment. Reflective exercises must end with action, whether that's as simple as rewriting a process that goes into a team manual or as involved as restructuring positions and responsibilities. To say that you learned from failure has little meaning. To learn and then apply those learnings with thoughtful change does.

You can't hold your people accountable if you don't do the same for yourself. Every leader requires think time in a day—uninterrupted time detached from the myriad details of daily demands that provides the space to see the larger terrain of company trajectory. And every leader requires reflection time in a day—about the day's events, about the status of projects, and about our own actions, behaviours, obsessions, and blind spots. Think time and reflection time are not identical, even if they spring from similar sources. Reflection includes a will to admit our little daily failures (and our big ones) and to share what we learn from those with our team. Our willingness to be open about the growth that emerges from our shortcomings will go a long way toward changing the larger culture around us. And give yourself a break. A leader can't be everything to everyone. Remember that on some days, good enough is good enough. Tomorrow you'll again set your sights high.

We need to learn to be honest with ourselves about our own proclivities and about our strengths and weaknesses. For example, one thing I know about myself is that I get so energized about new ideas that I can get caught up in them, push people too hard, and want to race forward. Part of recognizing when to curb my enthusiasm comes in learning to respect the differences in others. Much of my job is listening to the smart ideas, expertise, and inventiveness of others around me and encouraging a coordinated and cohesive path forward for the company that all can get excited about. Sometimes that means selling an idea, and sometimes it means recognizing when I'm out ahead of the company's capabilities. Sometimes it means admitting I'm wrong, and sometimes it means I need to retool how I present an idea so that others can see it in a new light. Most often it means finding common ground and then working collaboratively to refine the idea. Once a project is in motion, the key is that I get out of the way to provide room for my team to create a sense of ownership. I need them each doing what they do best. If I've approached my leadership role in the right way, I've been careful to get the right people in the right positions, and we've created a culture where once something gets the green light, they exert control over their portion of the necessary work.

I am convinced that when we create cultures of open communication and supported collaboration, people learn not to take things personally and work collectively. I'm also convinced that the stronger the collective ownership of a project or strategy, the more colleagues will hold one another accountable.

Expectations about accountability, like those about striving for excellence, have to be present at every level and in every layer of your enterprise. These ideas don't just apply to those in senior positions or even just to those with management responsibilities. If these traits aren't present in your managers, they're almost certain to be lacking among your frontline teams. Often the only personal contact your customer has is with the front line. They are the ones who leave a lasting impression. What do you expect of that impression? Can you realistically expect excellence or hold them accountable to high standards unless they feel that they are heard, believe that they are genuinely perceived as vital to the company mission, and see evidence that hard work, continued education, and sustained excellence can allow them to rise within the company? Because we want our teams to strive for excellence, we must engage them, treat them with respect, and recognize their contributions. If we lead a company where the frontline team member who shows ambition, pride in work, and a will to further their education is provided the opportunity to advance into a management position, we will create a team member who feels a sense of ownership in the company, and we'll have a model others look to as inspiration for their own advancement. When we acknowledge excellence in those who go beyond the expectations of their jobs or who demonstrate the sincerity of their caring for customers with public recognition before their peers, we'll see excellence repeated. When we have managers who demonstrate simple human touch and attend an event that is meaningful to a team member's life—a graduation ceremony, a child's hockey game, a funeral—they cement a respect and a sense of belonging that changes their team member's perception of their employer and their job.

Lastly, I am convinced that people are motivated by improving themselves, by improving the lives of others, and by contributing to lasting change. If we lead organizations that share those values, then our people will want to be part of moving the organization in positive directions. It's human nature to try to become the best version of ourselves possible. There's no reason we cannot harness striving for excellence and apply it to the companies for which we work.

# WHAT HAVE YOU DONE TO PROPEL YOUR PEOPLE TOWARD EXCELLENCE?

It's easy to say that you want your company and the people in it to strive for excellence, but what measures do you have in place to make sure that it's more than talk?

- What's your own perception of failure? Have you broadcast that perception into your company?

- When you hear grumbling around the watercooler, how do you react?

- Have you incorporated reflection time into your daily schedule? Have you created processes that ensure similar reflection time is built into your projects, your team meetings, and your employees' self-review?

- How do you measure success? What incentives do you provide for those who meet those measures?

# CHAPTER 11

# Establish Equilibrium: Exceeding Expectations while Maintaining the Mission

At its centre, a leader's role is to reduce risks and identify opportunities, which then enables us to be excellent allocators of financial and human capital. Too much focus on one aspect of the business and another suffers. To be successful as a leader, achieving equilibrium on multiple fronts is key. Because I love to ski, thinking about acquiring the balance needed for successful leadership makes me imagine the approaches you have to learn in order to ski steep, difficult terrain gracefully. As we've all experienced through our careers and even more clearly through the age of COVID-19, in business leadership it often feels like the visibility on the ski slope is poor, there may well be hidden obstacles in the snow, the weather is constantly changing, and rather than having the balancing aid of poles in your hands, it can feel like you're juggling several balls. While skiing is an individual sport, business success is a team game, so picture that steep terrain and then imagine trying to get your entire workforce pointed downhill and skiing with enough unison that they aren't bumping into one another, all with the aim of everyone arriving at a preselected destination at the same time. How's this possible? It's going to take clear communication to point out the dangers, reaching out to one another where the visibility is poor, and caring about our teammates enough that we help each other up when we fall. Everyone on the team has to know where the destination is located, even if no one individual has the one map that will ensure arrival. It certainly helps if everyone agrees that the destination is one worth reaching.

On the ski mountain, that destination may be a cozy lodge and a hot toddy. The agreed-upon destination in business can be balanced on two fronts—arrival at completion of a phase in a strategic plan and continued fulfillment of larger mission-driven objectives. At Revera, we are intentional in establishing five-year business goals. The route to achieving them always contains unexpected obstacles, but our track record at reaching business goals has been strong. Part of equilibrium is doing so in a manner that preserves purpose. In the current five-year cycle, the need to preserve purpose during COVID-19 has severely disrupted the business plan. But to ignore purpose would have been unthinkable.

The good news is that we can learn balance. In fact, maintaining equilibrium in a wide variety of responsibilities is both a skill a leader has to learn and a strategy for guiding our companies forward. We'll talk about several important points of equilibrium over the course of this chapter. All are tools for establishing the big equilibrium that is the focus of the book: balancing profit and purpose. In the last chapter, I discussed a critical approach that represents another core mechanism for getting there: balancing high expectations and accountability. In this chapter, I'll share some of the approaches I use to try to maintain balance across a variety of terrain for myself as a leader.

# The Nature of Equilibrium

Balance starts with the central ideas that I've used to create the major divisions in the book: Never lose sight of natural inquisitiveness and embrace courageous curiosity in learning new things about our businesses and about the larger world; apply innovation to find new solutions in order to take our businesses in new directions that are fitting for their strengths, consistent with their mission, and necessary for market demands; and invest energy in cultivating a productive, desirable, respectful culture within our businesses that allows flexibility while creating stability. Remove one of these core elements and we will never achieve equilibrium between profit and purpose. The path to achieving each of these three elements is found in following our human instincts to do the right thing. That moral compass can become our key balancing aid, our virtual ski poles, if you will. Lean too exclusively toward purpose, and we may no longer have a sustainable business venture at all; lean too far toward profit, and we'll likely have a business that's not worth sustaining because it is morally corrupt.

Applying the principles I address in this chapter is kind of like skiing—on the tough days, you get back to the basics you learned in your youth and apply the experience you have picked up from those foundations. Like all things, leading takes practice. Eventually balance comes more naturally. With concerted effort and application over time, you learn how to become balanced within yourself, which will help you make balanced decisions that accomplish good for the entire organization.

## ACHIEVING LEADERSHIP EQUILIBRIUM

- Apply inquisitiveness.
- Seed innovation.
- Invest in the people, values, and ideas that align with the organization's mission.

Because I lead a company that is dedicated to serving the needs of a vulnerable population, alignment with mission always means making decisions that further the interests of our residents in ways that take their needs seriously and treat their lives with the individual dignity and respect they deserve. Revera's core mission is inherently a humanistic one where a focus on human interests, values, and dignity predominates.

Treating our business as a humanistic enterprise, even if it is the natural bearing to which our compass points, isn't the only part of our business we've got to get right. A business focused on caring for others is still a business. All businesses, whether they are private, public, or not-for-profit, need to create sustainability by managing resources. The main difference is simply where earnings are distributed. Our size, financial investment, and the organizational infrastructure that keeps us in business allow us to impact the quality of life for our residents at levels and in ways a nonprofit never could. Your specific challenges may be different from Revera's, but the broader pattern, those vital elements of sustainable and ethical business practice—don't skimp on quality, don't betray your values, don't treat customers and team members as disposable—are the same as ours. So are the pressures you face from your board and your shareholders. So let's start there with the steep and deep terrain, because if you can get comfortable with the hardest balance points, the rest can be mastered with comparative ease.

Bear with me while I take you back to skiing for a moment. We've all seen beginner skiers (and if you ski, you were one once). Their skis are splayed wide, forming a "pizza slice," like they are trying to remove all the snow from the mountain. They are off-balance, leaning impossibly far forward on their skis on the verge of losing control. They don't trust their ski edges. Poles seem hazards rather than helpful tools. They haven't learned the power and control that comes with subtle shifts of weight.

One of the first things you learn in a ski lesson is to paint, mentally, the ski slope in front of you with an imaginary vertical line—the fall line. The fall line is the path of least resistance, the line a snowball would take (or you will if you fall). As your skiing improves, you learn to keep your shoulders pointed down the fall line while you turn your legs across it, which allows your edges to grab the snow and control your speed while maintaining your balance. In business, that line is the balance point between the core values driving the mission of your company and your responsibility to provide financial return to your shareholders. The fall line does not represent a division; it represents a point of equilibrium. Lean too far into one leg, and you'll need to transfer some weight to your other leg to maintain balance and control speed. Forget the fundamentals of weight transfer, and you'll find yourself shooting straight down the fall line out of control. In a business application, poles become the tools of innovation and technology. Edges become the structures of adaptability and change management. Dependence on core strength and vertical alignment over your skis becomes core values and corporate environment that allows you to control speed and direction.

Allow me to illustrate what I mean. In the case of Revera, the first wave of COVID-19 meant acknowledging we had to shift our balance and accept that a commitment to resident health meant directing substantial financial resources into ensuring their protection and that of our team members. As the crisis deepened, we knew we would face a significant period when we had to shift away from the normal financial controls and oversight of the business. Sometimes simply doing the right thing to adhere to your mission means acknowledging that your bottom line has to take a major hit. But it doesn't have to mean falling down in a spectacular crash of spilled gear and broken bones. With creativity, innovation, and the backbone of an effective culture that keeps team members strongly committed, any crisis can be weathered.

> **With creativity, innovation, and the backbone of an effective culture that keeps team members strongly committed, any crisis can be weathered.**

To ski steep terrain, you've not only got to commit to the individual turn but also to a whole series of turns after that. Sound familiar? If you simply bomb straight down the fall line, you'll crash. If you give into fear and lurch to a precarious stop while gravity tries to pull you downhill, well, there you are, not going anywhere while your fear only builds. Business decisions require a similar balance between risk and reward, moving the enterprise forward by overcoming fear. We practice our due diligence but don't allow ourselves to become frozen in the face of a difficult decision. You can't stand on the slope forever while your competitors pass you by, but the more you know about the terrain ahead, the better. Let's face it, however—you can't know everything that awaits you.

With the twists and turns of COVID-19, even as we made necessary decisions in the moment, we had to know that the crisis stage would not last forever. There would be many more turns to reach the bottom, but we had to navigate a course even when we couldn't see the end. It started by accepting that COVID-19 was our reality for the foreseeable future, then setting priorities for how we would create the safest possible living environments and ensure that we could meet our residents' medical and mental health needs. But as soon as we took the necessary actions, we also had to begin planning for the near- and the long-term future. It meant studying our reactions to the crisis and archiving our learnings in a manner that we could apply them to new problems that would inevitably arise in the future. Simultaneously, we had to find a path to get back to the concept of business sustainability.

Embracing the research conducted by the leading epidemiologists around the world and at home in Canada, we prepared for a second wave of COVID-19 by developing the pandemic response plan I have referenced from the outset of this book. The specialists who formed the External Advisory Committee provided the expertise to produce a multifaceted approach for forming best practices for combating COVID-19. It drew on expertise in data analytics, building design, clinical and operational processes and procedures, and workforce management. Revera shared our processes, procedures, policies, and general operational approaches with these experts as together we sought a plan D.

The Revera leadership team began implementing measures to respond to findings in the report. At the same time, we began developing strategic business plans in reaction to the financial shortfalls the company and its various investment partners suffered from pandemic shortages and expenditures. On the mission front, we recognized that the senior living sector needs to address existing, long-standing challenges and emerge from the pandemic stronger. Revera was, and is, committed to being part of the solution and investing in research, planning, and best practice designs that can drive lasting change in the industry. We communicated our will to work with all operators, governments, experts, and stakeholders to protect residents and prepare team members. We responded to the pandemic response plan's findings by focusing on action items like improving and developing executable best practices for infection prevention and control; screening, testing, and tracing; building design standards and physical facility improvements; recruitment, retention, and labour strategies; research opportunities for treatments and vaccines; and rethinking the range of senior living options. Similarly, to gain insight into the impact of COVID-19, we employed our partnerships with a number of our investment and management partners in order to assess the best strategies for carrying the business into the future, identifying portions of the business that produce the greatest profitability, markets that hold the greatest potential for growth, investment opportunities that emerged during the pandemic, and other opportunities.

We determined both mission-driven and business-driven objectives by applying robust data and concrete learnings developed throughout the greater organization. For example, using our partnership with Accenture, we were able to conduct deep analyses of proprietary data from more than 180 long-term care and retirement homes serving 20,000 residents across Canada. The analyses enhanced our understanding of the correlation between the occurrence, spread, and severity of COVID-19 outbreaks and clinical, operational, building/structural, and geographic contexts and guided our future actions, including adoption of enhanced screening, testing, and tracing practices at all sites. We hired additional infection prevention and control specialists and further expanded the company's already robust PPE strategy. To better track clinical data, Revera engaged HealthConnex to use its cloud-based Infection Control and Outbreak Management software in our operations. HealthConnex reduces the time needed by team members to collect and report on infection control-related data. Designed specifically for senior living facilities, it incorporates the use of innovative mobile apps to collect hand hygiene data and signs and symptoms data to help improve resident safety. HealthConnex allows our team members to capture and report on information, including infection cases, laboratory results, hand hygiene audits, immunization, and antibiotic and multidrug-resistant organism history as part of the clinical care planning process. Partnering with such robust and niche-focused companies is a prime example of how investment in innovation can be a powerful way to solve problems and achieve balance.

Something as complex and as life threatening as COVID-19 really demonstrates why you have to develop systematic approaches to problem-solving that are deeply creative and groundbreaking. When you face a virus that threatens the people you have dedicated your career to serving, you have to come together as innovative teams. Using efforts learned after the first wave of COVID-19 now allowed us to reach near 80 percent accuracy in predicting where outbreaks would occur, differentiating between which sites are most susceptible to a large spread, and forecasting an outbreak's duration. We were able to assess where broader community spread events were likely to occur, providing us a better ability to adapt stricter measures as needed.

By being nimble, we were able to take action on our learning. The other result was that we were better positioned to move from crisis response to stabilization mode. It's not as if the complex functions of running a large corporation stopped because there was a pandemic. Because we are a company that has followed the tenets I have outlined in this book to the very best of our ability (notice I say best, not perfect), we were able to learn from crisis and still move forward.

That is no small challenge. As a company you have to stay viable. To do that, sometimes trying to do the right thing is quite painful. To meet the safety and logistical demands of COVID-19, we had to expend a great deal of capital on non-revenue-generating aspects of the business. That outflow of capital has made us re-examine parts of the business strategy, some that were already under scrutiny and some that were not.

## Balancing What's Out of Control with What You Can Control

True to the nature of unpredictability, fallout from COVID-19 took another form in 2021. I would use the phrase "unexpected fallout," and in many ways this is true, although with the benefit of hindsight, I suppose you can see much of what happened as the pandemic waged on as an inevitable, if regrettable, chain of events. While nearly every aspect of the COVID-19 virus was an unknown as it began its spread across the globe, we did know, based on the nature of coronavirus infections historically, that the elderly and the immunocompromised were going to be the most susceptible to infection. What we didn't know then was that when community transmission of the virus occurred, including among asymptomatic individuals, it was nearly impossible to keep the virus out of that community's congregate living residences. This was as true for university dorms as it was for senior long-term care homes, with one critical difference: universities could, and did, send their students home. That's obviously not an option for seniors. Because of the manner in which COVID-19 preys upon the biological vulnerability of the elderly, in locations where community transmission was present, residents in Revera homes died during the pandemic, despite the heroic efforts of our teams to keep the virus in check. Their deaths were tragic and weighed upon all of our team members. Given what we learned months after the first appearance of COVID-19 through global research and data analysis by epidemiologists, the concentration of so many deaths of seniors living in congregate settings worldwide may seem inevitable. This was particularly true in Ontario and Quebec, where the virus was sweeping through urban centres faster than health organizations and provincial governments could act, its very presence in the places family and team members had to frequent to conduct the ordinary parts of their daily lives a threat to our residential homes.

What may seem equally inevitable, given the litigious nature of our society, a handful of families filed lawsuits against Revera, claiming we did not do enough to protect their loved ones. And in what I would label as a third inevitability, the media went into a frenzy reporting on deaths in congregate living environments while showing little factual accuracy or depth of contextualized reportage. No one wants their business portrayed inaccurately in the media, much less in so negative a light. Optics matter in every business. Bad press can ruin a reputation, and few people have access to the actual facts if those facts are not reported by the media. An inaccurate perception of a business can be shaped by those who have little understanding of it and who possess little nuance. We are all consumers of media, and too often we are all guilty of accepting media stories as wholly factual. We seldom have the time or access to more carefully researched publications or to apply our own fact-checking. Naively, we assume all media outlets present factual, painstakingly reported news.

In the aftermath of the first wave of COVID-19, Revera was sometimes presented as a heartless corporation that mistreated its residents. Nothing could be further from the truth. Yet some media outlets fueled this perception. When families who had loved ones living in our residences praised our response to the pandemic and highlighted how much their family members valued Revera's loving and capable teams, somehow those stories were rarely aired. Meanwhile, our frontline teams, exhausted from overwork and emotionally drained by maintaining excellence during challenging circumstances in locked-down residences, faced inaccurate media depictions of workplaces they valued. They did so even while trying to balance home lives where their children were tasked with learning remotely and their own vulnerable family members needed protection. As a result of a media frenzy, I and some of my senior leadership team received death threats.

Continued change is inevitable, and the future repercussions of the COVID-19 virus on the senior living sector are likely to be significant. Much remains unknown. Reacting to the unknown, and in order to cope with ongoing change, we immediately began restructuring parts of the business, including consolidating management of our investments into one corporate division. All in all, the degree of change required through this chain of events is a good reminder that even leaders at the highest levels of an organization have other forces to which they answer. It's also good evidence for why leadership requires imaginative problem-solving in rapidly shifting business environments. Without adhering to the principles we've used to guide creation of the culture we established at Revera, we might not have had the ability to adapt as circumstances required.

The decisions forced by this set of circumstances have not been easy. Each one has a cost. Moving out of the long-term care sector will have a profound impact on our people. While the long-term care portion of the business accounts for a small percentage of our profits, fulfilling its demanding mission requires nearly half of our workforce. There's nothing that tugs at a business leader's humanity more than the thought of having to let people go. In the long-term care portion of the business, as we are successful in selling those assets to other providers, the impact on frontline team members should be nearly invisible. By working though several of the partnerships we've used to expand the reach of the organization, we have tried to identify buyers who share Revera's values. In the best-case scenarios, a sale will mean little more than a different corporate name on a former team member's pay cheque. Of course, in a business as large in scale and complex as ours, a great deal of dedicated support for that portion of the business occurs in our central office, and a divestment of those parts of the business will make a number of positions unnecessary. As I write this portion of the book, Revera remains in a fluid situation, but we are fortunate that team reduction is minimal. To be blunt, this reality is a reminder that some things about being a leader just suck. It's a simple, if unwanted, reminder that all leaders must establish another balance, that rising high in an organization can have a lot of intellectual rewards, but the responsibilities of our positions simultaneously produce a lot of psychological stress. Hard decisions go with the terrain.

In a dream world, no Revera resident or team member would have ever contracted COVID-19, and certainly no one would have died. In a dream world, no one would lose their jobs. We don't live in dream worlds. That simple reality points to another important equilibrium. It would be negligent to ignore that COVID-19 deaths occurred in our residences. It's prudent to try to find out why, determine whether there were measures we could have taken unilaterally to prevent them, and get to work in partnership with others on measures that were beyond our control, like lobbying for provincial governments to treat congregate senior living residences with the same status as health system facilities when encountering future community health emergencies. The desire part of me wishes we had the capacity to upgrade all of the oldest properties within our residential portfolio. Simple economics reminds us that we have to follow a data-driven, systematic approach that prioritizes the order of such redevelopment in a manner that accounts for demographic and market needs.

In a similar manner, we must identify where growth in a particular market can improve profitability and generate investable capital that can fuel targeted redevelopment. Because substantial parts of our central office are focused on aspects of the business that are not directly associated with frontline support, even as the pandemic moved on from its first wave, we were able to see and seize business opportunities. Because of analysis we had initiated eighteen months prior to the pandemic, we were able to start the process for a new acquisition in 2020, a well-located, well-constructed community that we believe we can run better than its current owner, one that met all the criteria our analysis had employed.

Whether we were investing in new measures to protect resident health or new business ventures, learning to go forward meant learning from past experiences. The most important learnings come when gravity is trying to pull you off-balance.

# Some Principles of Applied Equilibrium

What are some ways to achieve this kind of balance we were able to employ during a time of crisis?

*Balancing timeliness and informed decisions*: We can't wait forever to make decisions by falling victim to analysis paralysis, but we do need a plan. Bombing down the fall line is the fastest way down the slope; it's also the best way to hurt yourself or someone else. I gather all the information I can but stick to a timeline. In the heat of a crisis, speed matters, but blind, reactive decisions usually cause more problems than they solve. You don't have to know everything. I've learned to balance the unknown with the known, and that allows me to differentiate instinctual responses that reflect my values from impulsive ones. Considering the impacts of decisions on people doesn't have to mean allowing emotion to interfere with good analysis. If a media story has you angry or you're disappointed in a team member, those are moments when your human response gets in the way. Even in times of crisis that require rapid response, if we're running our organizations right, we've already been building strategic response plans into the culture. We've not only groomed a team to think ahead and practice nimble pivots but also developed a culture where we can adapt to the specific, unknown circumstances because we've been planning for the unexpected. In reality, we're either in the midst of, or planning for, transformation nearly all the time. When the mountain slope before you looks impossible, take a few deep breaths, get back to basics, and focus on as many turns as you can see ahead. Fear will only get in the way of completing those turns.

*Balancing multiple perspectives*: We must have the ability to readjust our perspectives to solve problems. The view from the chairlift—that high-elevation, overarching strategic view—gives us one perspective. The view from the ground—digging into the details of an operation, studying the micro-data—provides another. I expand my perspective by listening to others who are well placed to provide me points of view I might not naturally consider or have access to on my own. Reading the snow and weather forecast is useful, as is talking with the ski patrollers who laid down the first runs that morning. Every perspective I'm provided helps me achieve balance. You can see some of the terrain from above the run, but let's face it—a lot of it just looks white. I use the perspective gained and the information provided to expand my thinking. I'm seeking input, not asking for position papers. I weigh the information I receive and then trust my experience and my instincts. Until your skis meet the snow, you can't know its texture or its moisture content or its layers.

*Balancing personal vision and an informed view*: Just as you can't make purely emotional decisions, you need to solicit the opinions and harvest the knowledge base of your team but ultimately trust (and own) your vision. Ask five quality skiers for the best line through a challenging mogul field and you may get five opinions. Learn to listen to the reasoning behind the line they recommend and then ask what alternatives they've tried. Their opinions matter little; the rationale behind those opinions matters a great deal. When you are curious about your world and regularly ask the interesting questions that tug at you, you're not only better informed but also a better critical thinker. Especially in a time of crisis, you can't take the information you're fed at face value. You've got to be good at soliciting the knowledge and opinions of your experts, be prudent on getting your senior leaders to gather information and apply their skills and experience, and then be adept at synthesizing what you learn. You have to recognize that there will always be filters present in the points of view you hear. Your CFO will see things differently from your COO because they are trained to do so. Some will, consciously or unconsciously, work to protect the interests they represent. As a result, what you learn won't be perfect. You've got to balance point of view with the facts provided. You need to have a rapid and finite open discussion with your leaders about what, collectively, you do know. And then you've got to make decisions and own those decisions. Sometimes people just need you to tell them to go left or right. When a squirrel tries to cross a road, if they are indecisive at the critical moment, they may become a flat squirrel.

*Balancing getting it right and getting it done*: The decisions we reach won't be perfect. As we discussed in the last chapter, I try to build teams that want to aim high but teach them that they have to join together to move the organization forward in a clear and focused direction. There will always be adjustments needed along the way. Even when the weather is clear and visibility is good, if you're skiing an open, fast cruising run and you can see every turn in your mind before you make it, somewhere there's going to be an icy patch that will throw you off your line. You get through the tricky turn as best you can by falling back on good habits developed over hundreds of previous runs and then you adjust to get back on your line.

During the early stages of COVID-19, we had to isolate residents to protect them. Actions like closing communal dining rooms affected the logistics of mealtimes and personnel needs for meal delivery. Group events became personal experiences; coordinated transportation for resident errands now required team members to take on additional tasks. Every action required more time and more team members. The impacts affected our team members and our residents, disrupting everyone's lives. We adjusted accordingly, using team member tools we'd already put in place to help manage and communicate needs. But some team members needed to step away from their roles to care for children or other family. Some feared for their own health.

Needing teams to wear PPE slowed and complicated everything. Yet one of our greatest roadblocks was put in place by unions representing some of our workers. Union officials took intractable positions against commonsense adjustments to worker contracts, so much so that they made it nearly impossible for some of our team members to work at all, jeopardizing their pay cheques. The impacts on our team members' lives risked those of the residents they cared for. With time and thoughtful negotiation, we found a path forward, but the circumstance was a reminder that despite our best planning, the immediate problems we must solve often originate from sources we can't see "under the snow." Did we get all the logistical challenges right? No. But we had put systems in place that allowed for flexibility, and whenever we encountered excellent, creative solutions among our team members, we replicated them elsewhere. Encouraging learning and creativity, developing processes to meet change, and trusting the people-focused culture we'd developed over time allowed us to get things done in a manner that never lost sight of the impacts on our residents' well-being.

*Balancing resources*: When the unexpected arrives and you implement plan D, often you must reallocate resources, both financial and human capital, in order to preserve the long-term interests and reputation of your organization. I've rarely skied a day where weather, snow conditions, terrain, and my personal biorhythms didn't demand changes in attire or equipment, like swapping sunglasses for goggles or adding a balaclava. The wise skier dresses in layers or what my German friends used to call peels. Think of such layers as tools to meet changing conditions. In business, having tools in capital investments and flexibility within teams allows you to reposition money and people when circumstances require. Just as you need access to financial liquidity to meet sudden expenditure needs, you must create teams capable of rapidly shifting application of their expertise to new projects. This is as true when a crisis arises as it is when an opportunity presents itself. If you have too much bureaucracy within individual teams and in your larger organizational structure, you're too slow to pivot. Your teams need to be specialized enough that you eliminate redundancy in the organization but adaptable such that they don't become locked into the belief that they do only one thing well. This need lends more support to the reason that while your leaders must have a working understanding of products and processes used by their teams, they must also be generalists who work across those teams and across the larger organization, putting the knowledge of their experts to work for the company. Only then can they direct rapid transitions when needs or opportunities warrant reorientation of resources.

*Balancing communication flow*: Transparency in communication, both inside the organization and externally, matters, yet there are always concerns about making certain those who need information can access it easily without being overwhelmed by an abundance of offerings. Nearly always there's a need to correct misinformation presented by the media or within parts of a large organization, whether accidental or malicious, without responding to every little detail that those outside the communications team develop. When a leader is misquoted or an internal memo that does not offer full context for an ongoing communication is shared in the media, it can resemble that feeling you get when your skis appear to get out ahead of you. Clear, factual communication always matters but rises to greater scrutiny during tumultuous times.

During the first wave of COVID-19, as soon as the virus crept into one Revera residence in British Columbia, the media began reporting sensationalized, inaccurate stories accusing us of neglecting our residents. Nonfactual reporting fueled rumors and frightened families. We'd long had an outstanding professional communications team in place that had always been central to our mission. In another equilibrium test, our communications team had to balance outbound information to correct misinformation circulating in the media with critical inbound information for our residents, their families, and our team members about necessary changes to protocols and their impacts on daily resident life. They had to calm the frenzy that is such a part of modern for-profit media while maintaining their role in coordinating necessary information across the entire organization, stretching our resources at an already stressful time. Both mattered immensely to the central mission of the company and to sustaining its reputation of excellence. It meant balancing the use of communication to heal in the moment and to prevent harm in the future. The antidote in both instances was speaking the truth. Of course, in a postfactual world, speaking truth can sometimes feel agonizingly ineffective, yet doing so is vital. It's always a delicate balancing act to know when not to engage with sensationalized reporting that is not well sourced, when to respond with formal statements offering accurate information, and when to personalize media relations by having leaders sit for interviews and similar engagements. We opt for transparency. That fact is embodied by how we opened company records to the pandemic review panel and how we made its findings publicly available. Sadly, offering factual transparency isn't always meaningful to those who have an existing agenda, but sharing facts whenever it doesn't threaten a resident's or a team member's privacy remains the best course of action. That includes admitting mistakes. None of us are perfect, so mistakes will happen. If we own up to them and then share the actions we've taken to avoid the same mistakes in the future, we not only are more likely to address a communication need but also will truly be bettering the organization.

*Balancing investment risk and reward*: At Revera, we made a five-year, $20 million commitment to invest in innovation that can have direct benefit to our residents. While $20 million is no small investment, it is placed on companies that have higher risk profiles because they are start-ups or they focus on new technologies or because they aren't always companies that can be scaled exponentially. All such investments are risk/reward calculations that are not entirely unlike the process you undertake at the top of a ski mountain. In my case, I'm not a young skier anymore. I work out regularly to stay in shape, but my body will tell me if I'm pushing my limits. While skiing, particularly as you get a bit wiser, you're doing risk assessment all the time. How difficult is the terrain? Are there visible hazards? Has weather affected visibility? Is the run crowded, and is there a mix of skier abilities that can produce more accidents? These numerous skiing questions have nearly literal business counterparts. Is there visible risk? Will other players impact the investment? Are market conditions likely to change? How complete and accurate is the information that's available?

The major partnerships we form are assessed not only in terms of stability and whether we make for a good fit but also for what the partner can bring to the table that we can't, whether that's an existing presence in a market we'd like to enter or access to products and services that will help us grow. When we're investing in smaller start-ups and entrepreneurs, certainly we look for those that have growth capacity, but sometimes we'll invest simply because we see that they can offer an improved quality of life for our residents. Typically, these sorts of investments support the central theme of this book, balancing profit with purpose. You might recall products I've shared like motion-activated safety lighting in resident apartments or application-based communication and reservation systems—products that enrich our residents' lives and make us more competitive. Carefully chosen investments can transform the experiences of residents, their families, and the communal spaces they call home. Some smaller investments may not be the sort we anticipate will skyrocket, but a slow and steady adoption within a growing demographic can sometimes be an important strategy as well. When compared to what we might invest in a single major development, where we might have capital outlays from $500 million to approaching $1 billion of equity, some entrepreneurial investments are small, but we've had a good track record helping fund small companies early in their growth

> **Never discount the intangibles, whether that is your corporate reputation or the power of people willing to share their experiences about working with you.**

cycle. Indeed, that's a small component of why we make such investments. Such investing has a secondary effect and helps position us so that people are attracted to come work for us, form partnerships with us, or recognize our sincerity in trying to improve life experiences and consider coming to live in one of our residences. Our investments demonstrate our commitment to being a dynamic, forward-thinking business. They provide tangible and intangible benefits to us as a business, and many of those benefits have meaningful impact over the long term. Never discount the intangibles, whether that is your corporate reputation or the power of people willing to share their experiences about working with you.

*Balancing growth and dividends*: The investment decisions behind collaboration or funding with other companies are part of a larger strategy that must necessarily flux with both external and internal conditions. A big part of senior leaders' responsibilities includes advising their board on when it is time to return profits to the business to sustain growth and when it is wise to place profits into dividends. Just as there are periods during a long ski day when either changing mountain conditions or your own fitness can determine whether you are wise to push hard on a run or be a bit more protective against injury, there are a lot of conditions that determine when it's time to go fast or pull back on business growth. Either path can create important value. But you've got to be extremely thoughtful, apply the best-quality analytics available, assess the company's strategic vision, and be hypervigilant about communicating with individual board members and senior executives as you make and implement such decisions. Like all such decisions, they are not made in a static environment, and what may be best for the company this year (or sometimes this month) won't necessarily be repeated two years from now. Recognizing such dynamics is precisely a part of why trying to attain balance matters so greatly.

# A Key Equilibrium: Innovation and Infrastructure

Discussing critical investment decisions makes me mindful of another ongoing equilibrium discipline that has been central to my thinking in writing this book—creating a company that is driven by an entrepreneurial spirit but that possesses the infrastructure, organizational capabilities, and discipline of an established professional business. Part of what excited me as I took on leadership challenges over my career continues to excite me when we invest in entrepreneurs with great new products, services, or ideas. Along with their ability to move fast, their potential for growth and, most of all, their passion are hallmarks of great entrepreneurs. All good innovative products and services solve problems. And that's a basic need of all organizations that keeps me enthused to get up every day and go to work—a fascination with solving complex problems with our teams.

Often, however, entrepreneurs are still early in their development. Their companies still need to mature beyond innovative ideas and into the organizational and business development capacities required for sustained growth and expansion. A lot of entrepreneurs are like a lot of our youngest team members—idealistic and driven. Both are great qualities, as are passion, dedication, and resilience, which are common to entrepreneurs. They are all part of the reason there is a joy in mentoring innovators. But these qualities need to be partnered with farsightedness in strategic vision, an understanding of operating systems and effective corporate structure, a comprehensive understanding of complex markets, and direct experience managing large, dispersed workforces. Establishing equilibrium means shaping a company's culture so that it creates systems that are robust and sophisticated enough to be effective when scaled into sizable, multifaceted entities while still possessing the nimble, enthusiastic problem-solving qualities of the entrepreneur. If you'll permit me to return to my skiing metaphor one more time, it's kind of like hitting the steep, difficult terrain with the knowledge of a fifty-year-old who has been skiing every day of his life and who can afford the most technically advanced gear *and* the strong knees, musculature, and fearlessness of an eighteen-year-old.

Like all entrepreneurs, I've never had the luxury of having just one project as the sole focus of my attention. As leaders, we've got a lot of balls in the air while we're skiing down our fictional mountain. Sometimes I struggle to be honest with myself and practical when it comes to identifying those projects and initiatives that need the bulk of my time and attention. I have to be intentional about identifying projects that will need a lot of personal oversight and those that I can hand off to others on my team. That can be hard because my enthusiasm can make me want to control the direction of a particular project. Once I can let go and find satisfaction in the outcome without getting wrapped up in the process, I still have to know which ones I need to check in on with regularity and those that I can watch from afar. You simply can't do it all, and the fastest way to burn out is to have so many projects that you think can only be successful with your personal involvement that you simply become overstretched and overwhelmed.

For me, achieving equilibrium is often finding that fulcrum between my inherent passion and pragmatism. Passion is absolutely a wanted thing in business. But alone, it's not enough. Whether you are trying to fire up your employees by playing on their enthusiasm or you are contemplating a new investment in innovative technology, you've got to also consider the most practical needs. It's kind of like cooking. You want the richness of flavour and the exoticism of a new, intriguing dish, but even the best ingredients and unbridled enthusiasm for cooking aren't sufficient if you aren't measuring your ingredients with care and being systematic about following the steps that have been carefully detailed in the recipe.

# Balancing IQ and EQ

Managing my desire to drive forward with certain initiatives requires me to truly assess organizational priorities and our capacity for change. In order to properly complete such an assessment, I must strive to establish equilibrium between my IQ and my EQ. In order to do that, particularly when I can see the value we can affect from a new deal, partnership, or innovation, I have to make it a habit to step back and also assess what the impact will be on the organization and our people. It's a bit like being fitted for glasses during an eye exam when the ophthalmologist provides you a series of lenses to determine your prescription. Each option alters the clarity of your vision in nuanced ways. The equivalent for a leader is trying on the lens of the various people you represent. I've got to think about the impact of actions on different segments of my team members, from front line to central office and in between. I stop and try to consider the view of our residents. Of their families. Of our shareholders, collectively and individually. The action of such thinking is in itself turning to my emotional quotient.

You regularly encounter situations that test your IQ and your EQ balance. A common one is when you find yourself with a difficult leader at an important position in your company. What do you do when you have a team member who is bright, confident, enthusiastic, and driven but who simply doesn't fit the cultural values you've worked so hard to cultivate? Maybe they are an ineffective manager who won't listen to their team or someone with great ideas but who can't get their ego out of the way when it comes to putting ideas into action. Maybe they are good with team members but don't really understand the larger company strategy. Perhaps they are good strategists but terrible communicators. Are their deficits the kinds of things that can be addressed with the right mentoring, coaching, or education? Or are they entrenched in their behaviours? We're all familiar with the round peg in a square hole reality of personnel at every level of our businesses and can often see how this phenomenon at high leadership levels can severely damage the company. Yet too often we are reluctant to make the hard decisions required to fix the problem. Our emotions cloud our intellect. But often, for the good of the organization, moving this kind of individual to another role that plays to their strengths can accomplish a lot of good. And sometimes, if they don't fit the culture, no matter the skill they might bring, their presence just is too toxic to overlook, and you've got to be willing to enable them to go be successful somewhere else.

Balancing IQ and EQ requires purposeful vulnerability. It can be difficult to share mistakes I've made, but with practice and time, I've learned to take a kind of pride in the learning scars I have earned over my career. We've all made mistakes. We've all learned lessons. A big part of EQ is seeing mistakes and lessons as learning opportunities. When you can admit that you're not perfect, it's a lot easier for team members to change how they see themselves as well. They're more willing to learn from experience and less likely to cover up the skills they need to develop. I remember speaking during my interview with Patrice Merrin, my board chair at CML Healthcare, when she asked me to describe some of my learning scars. It is useful to think back to the times in your career that may have been the hardest but from which you learned the most. Recalling difficult lessons learned is a fast track to humility. You have to be able to differentiate when projecting strength is a disguise for uncertainty and when doing so is meant to inspire confidence and engagement in the face of crisis. The members of your team will see through the former and find inspiration and motivation in the latter.

Critical balances that must be achieved in a company (or in yourself) aren't easy. The best executive education in the world won't be enough to prepare you to achieve such equilibrium. It means a lot of give and take, a lot of time getting on those skis and feeling the difference as you shift your weight. It takes time and experience. And it will take a concerted effort on your part.

Once equilibrium is achieved, it's a powerful thing. Good balance allows you to move your company forward, which is always the goal, just like reaching the bottom of the ski slope. When you're starting out, just getting down the hill might feel like all that matters, but with patience, practice, and experience, you not only learn how to arrive with style but also take great satisfaction in all the nuances of getting there with speed, precision, and grace.

Grace matters. Not for style points. Grace in business isn't the same as on the ski slope. In business, grace is about never forgetting your purpose. It's about joining forces with a team to create a culture you can all be proud of. The balance points I've discussed in this chapter, these yin and yang examples of dualism, are a fundamental trait of being human, central to our nature and to the nature of the companies we run. Just as we have to find equilibrium to keep our bodies healthy, the same goes for our organizations. At the end of the day, we're all in people businesses. If we want to become better leaders, we've got to start by becoming better humans.

# WHAT'S YOUR YIN AND YANG? HOW DOES YOUR COMPANY MAINTAIN EQUILIBRIUM?

- When you make critical decisions, how do you ensure that you consider the various points of view of all those impacted? Do you have mechanisms in place to consider the views and needs of your customers? Of your employees? Of your shareholders?

- How conscious are you of applying both your IQ and your EQ when facing difficult decisions?

- What is the role of innovation in your company for finding equilibrium between shareholder value and corporate vision?

- In times of crisis, where does your compass point first?

- What is the relationship in your own work life between maximizing curiosity and developing creative solutions?

- Which do you value more, speed or thoroughness, when it comes to implementing decisions? Do you see speed and thoroughness as polar opposites or points on a continuum?

- How do you approach managing opposing viewpoints among your leadership team when it comes to critical collaborative decisions?

# Create Change by Making a Difference

It shouldn't take a pandemic to make us human. It shouldn't take observing courage and resiliency in the face of death to make us take stock of our values. It shouldn't take a crisis to remind a business about why it is in business in the first place. I'd like to think that the core principles I have outlined in this book, many of them core principles of humanity, have consistently guided my decisions and approaches throughout my career. I have consistently tried to be the kind of leader I have advocated here, but like all humans, I have made mistakes along the way, there have been decisions I wish I could revisit, and I've had to do the best I was able in a given moment. I have tried to be steadfast in learning from the past. In that spirit, I do hope—as we all should—that I'm a better leader today than I was twenty years ago. I've certainly learned a great deal. I've been forced to learn even more and at an exponentially faster rate just over the period of writing this book. As I have shared, much of this book was written in the midst of the worst global pandemic in the last one hundred years, and a number of the examples of these business philosophies are drawn from my experiences leading a senior living sector corporation through COVID-19. Because this pandemic disproportionally affected seniors to the rest of the population, the experience offered stark lessons about the need for adaptability and resiliency. It also reminded all of us about maintaining humanistic priorities in business and about the value of *every* human life. I see COVID-19 as a useful catalyst for being mindful about adhering to our values and about developing the vision and support structure that can manage tectonic change.

I have always had huge empathy and respect for what our frontline care teams do to support our seniors who call Revera home; I now have a much more profound and empathetic understanding of the impact of that work and have witnessed their ability to adapt as circumstances warranted. There have been so many examples of selfless behaviour that make me exceptionally proud of all our operating teams across our various platforms and geographies in these challenging times. My pride is only intensified when I recognize that we have sought to maintain the independence and the dignity of our residents while also protecting them. That's been paralleled in our business model, for we've done everything we can to promote safety (we've done right), and we've come through intact, relevant, and stable so that we can continue to meet the needs of the future (we've done well).

The themes in this book are meant to highlight how leaders need to balance their intellect and their sense of purpose. I hope the book has successfully highlighted the human side of business, since business decisions in almost every case have a binary ROI element combined with the less measurable impact on people. The art with the science.

The other main theme pertains to strategy and planning. It is always important to have a clear purpose combined with boundaries on what you are about and what you are not about, what you are good at and what you are less good at. You can develop scenarios and alternatives, but what I've learned is you often have to take one step back or a step sideways to progress forward, and the path that you thought you might be on turns out to be slightly different than anticipated. Adaptability and balance are critical to success both in business and in life. It is a rare bird among all of us who is able to spot the exact path forward without working through some struggle and learning along the way. If you're not struggling, you're not learning. So learn to enjoy the struggle.

> **Adaptability and balance are critical to success both in business and in life.**

That's probably the most important balance we've achieved at Revera. For while it's absolutely true that Revera and our partners are in the caregiving business, it's a business and not a charity. We need to make sure we are sustainable over time. We'll continue to meet the needs of a growing senior demographic with excellence because we have strived to do right even as we do well. The professionalism we have reached in our company has fostered an ability to accomplish meaningful contingency planning quickly. Our adaptability has paid dividends. That adaptability has continued to be manifested by employing an open culture that promotes innovative problem-solving.

Have we gotten it perfect? Of course not. Nor will you. Even as we prepare to face facts revealed in the course of a pandemic—not the last pandemic we will face, I am sure, and certainly not our last tectonic shift—I gather learnings from how we have performed and am already thinking about changes that will be needed in the future. I give a great deal of attention to our cultural makeup that can enhance our ability to be thoughtful at the same time that we can be agile. Changing a culture is an evolution, not a revolution. The COVID-19 experience has only clarified the truth of such a statement. But I do think we've maintained a number of important

**Changing a culture is an evolution, not a revolution.**

equilibria over the course of this challenging disruption. How? I would remind you of some key concepts of this book that have held answers: finding ways to empower people (employees and customers alike) and acknowledging that accountability accompanies empowerment; encouraging curiosity, open communication, and collaboration while recognizing that action must emerge from discussion; fostering a culture that supports adaptability and innovation that never loses sight of our values and our mission.

If you are going to be able to create the kind of culture I've tried to illustrate within this book, it starts in one place: You must become comfortable in your own skin. You need to know who you are and know what you're good at while seeing where you need to learn. Companies need leaders who are confident but not egotistical, open to ideas but capable of making unwavering decisions, humane and empathetic while aware that the needs of the company can require difficult decisions. Agility starts with good balance. You can move quickly only when you're grounded and practiced. When you constantly face a changing world, it's these qualities that will allow you to take rapid assessments capable of producing speedy adaptations that will transfer agility into forward motion. The challenges are real, but challenge can be rewarding. No one ever suggested that guiding a company is easy. But the capacity you have to lead change in your company can also change lives for the better. That's a worthy goal. And remember, inside every challenge lies an opportunity.

# ABOUT THE AUTHOR

Tom Wellner is president and CEO of Revera Inc. Since joining Revera in 2014, Mr. Wellner has led the organization through significant transformational changes, developing the company's strategic direction to grow, innovate, and lead in the senior living sector. He has always desired to make a difference in the aging process, which is what excited him more than half a decade ago to make the shift into seniors' services and investments. As Revera's strategy continues to evolve into more of an investment management model with a foundation in the aging demographic, he leads the management of the partnerships Revera has across its operational, development, and investment network in Canada, the US, and the UK. Investments have grown Revera's portfolio to more than five hundred properties touching more than sixty-three thousand seniors and employing fifty-five thousand team members internationally, making it one of the largest in the world.

After an enjoyable early life in the Maritimes and following university, Wellner started his career at Eli Lilly, where he held a variety of global operational and leadership roles. In 2008, after finishing up at Lilly and a successful two decades in the global pharmaceutical and biotech industry, he began a journey to find the balance, meaning, and empathy in the businesses he has had the pleasure of leading. Mr. Wellner holds an Honours Bachelor of Science degree in life sciences from Queen's University and has completed the ICD Directors Education Program at Rotman School of Management as well as executive education through Harvard Business School. He sits on the boards of a number of public and private companies. He loves exploring and spending time with his wife, Mary, and their family, travelling when possible but especially enjoying time together at their summer cottage on Caledonia Island on Lake Rosseau.